A Policy of Hate

Douglas G. Beaudoin

ISBN: 1516993241
ISBN-13: 978-1516993246

DEDICATION

In Memory of World War II Veteran
Frank McGinley 1927 – 2004
USN Pacific Theater

ACKNOWLEGEMENTS

BOU MENG

"A SURVIVOR FROM KHMER ROUGE PRISON S-21"

TABLE OF CONTENTS

Introduction

World War II in Asia and the Pacific began as a result of the Sino-Japanese War in 1937 between China and Japan. Japan invaded Manchuria in 1931 and occupied the northern Provinces of China near Beijing. The United States, Britain and France condemned Japan for the invasion and instituted an oil embargo on Japan, which prompted Japan to bomb Pearl Harbor on December 7, 1941, in retaliation to the oil embargo, thus starting World War II in the Pacific.

After World War II, Indochina and Southeast Asia was given the opportunity to declare independence from colonial rule from Great Britain, Netherlands, France and the United States territory, the Philippines. China had fallen to communism in 1948, under the leadership of Mao Zedong, which set the stage for revolution in Indochina. Vietnam, under the leadership of Ho Chi Minh, elected to follow in the footsteps of Mao in an effort to organize a communist revolutionary army against the French occupation in Indochina. Vietnam would be divided into two separate nations, North and South in 1954.

The United States disliked colonialism and remained neutral during the beginning of the French Indochina war and even supported Ho Chi Minh's effort toward independence until it learned that Ho Chi Minh wanted to install a communist government. Cambodia and Laos was also under attack by communist insurgents which would eventually lead to U.S. involvement in Southeast Asia in an effort to stop the spread of communist through-out Asia and Indonesia.

This book is about the atrocities and the sinister policies implemented by those in power who orchestrated crimes against humanity and its people. Repressive regimes designed to eradicate those with differing social, religious, ethnic and contrasting ideologies were especially targeted. This is an un-sanitized version of Asia's modern history and the wars created for control of governments. It's about the policies that changed the lives of millions of innocent people both in Asia and those who fought in the wars to stop the spread tyranny. While much of the history in Asia and Indochina has been relegated to the back pages of newspapers, with the exception of Vietnam; millions of civilians died as a result of policies that were established for the single purpose of installing despot regimes and maintaining their perpetuity.

I have purposely avoided going into tedious detail about battles and strategies which can be a source for further reading for those who wish, but rather elected to focus on historical events that shaped certain events in modern Asian history. It is worth noting that the term "policy" is not confined to U.S. policy exclusively, but rather the policies of other Asian countries whose primary purpose was to spread the seed of hate towards a particular class of people. While many continue to deny their involvement, historical records and documentation counter their claims of innocents.

Even though the Vietnam War lasted nearly 20 years, China has been in a perpetual state of war for nearly 100 years. I have made an effort to document actual events, and purposely left-out many so that the reader wouldn't get "bogged" down in needless detail on names, dates and specific locations and dialog.

It is important to learn about modern history in Asia to help understand why leaders today react and respond to specific current events, such as the dispute over the islands in the South China Sea and President Obama's funding of $90 million in Laos over undetonated bombs during the secret war in Laos in the 1960's.

"It makes patriotism an excuse for carrying fire,
Pestilence, and famine into the lands;
It leaves to virtue nothing but the spirit of censoriousness."

"The Pleasures of Hating"
By Hazlitt

Chapter 1

The Spread of Communism in Asia

Something in a society happens that allows dictators, socialist and fascist to flourish. Most often the military has become so large and powerful that it destroys the very same government that created it. In most cases, countries become prone to have frequent Coup d'états that lacks a system of safeguards that protects the separation of power between the military and the civilian government. The usurper believes his destiny is to control the masses for the greater good of the people, which is seldom the case. The people are powerless to stop the transgressor and the tool he uses is propaganda and a self-styled ability to convince the people he is taking control government out of the necessity for peace. The traditional duties of the military are to thwart conflicts and invasions from foreign aggressors, but most often is to protect the regime against their own people.

Indochina and most of Asia is an agrarian society with strict traditional and religious principles and beliefs. Agriculture and in particular rice, is the main crop and primary food source in most Asian countries. For those who lived in the Golden Triangle, opium replaced rice as the cash crop for many ethnic groups in the region, but for the rural villagers, their economy was based primarily on farming. Since everyone in the village was in the same economic class, class struggle was nonexistent and unnecessary.

Over centuries of cultivation, much of the agricultural land was over cultivated by using the same crops over and over, thus depleted the vital nutrients in the soil for consistent crop yields. The forest provided natural foods for a subsistence and timber for building housing, shelters and fences for livestock and grain sheds. The forest and jungles of Asia are important for the rural farmer in supplementing their diet during periods of poor harvest. Bamboo from the jungle is still an essential building material throughout Asia. But, as the land became over cultivated, and over hunted, it became necessary to clear more land for agriculture, thus depleting much of forest land. By the end of the 20th century, 70% of the forests and 95% of the wildlife vanished from much of Asia, which forced the rural population to become even more dependent on government for subsidies.

In Asia, Europe and America, most rural farmers were forced to travel great distances for building materials, firewood and sell their farm products in the markets in the larger cities. Industrialization, and in particular the automobile, became an essential part of transporting supplies and products to markets, however, in less industrialized countries, such as Asia, it became a logistics problem of mass proportion, since most didn't own a vehicle and traveling using an ox cart was much too slow and impractical.

In Asia, it was basically a two class system, whereas 90 percent of the people were poor and 70 percent were farmers, while the rest were wealthy landlords and government officials. In some countries the government-owned the land and the peasant farmers paid the government a portion of their harvest as rent and taxes. What was left over, the farmers were allowed to keep. Under this type of feudal system, it is easy to understand how famine could occur if the farmer had a failed harvest, and the government and landlords demanded their cut of the harvest, leaving the farmer with nothing to carry the family through the winter. It was a classic feudal system common in early Europe and still continues today in poor countries around the world.

Other Asian countries allowed their citizens to own land and work their own farms; such was the case in early China before communism and before the collective farming system after the communist took over. But the farmer still needed money for seed, tools and personal items which couldn't be bartered.

Under normal situations, the farmer would barter for tools and basic staples such as rice, which was a desired commodity. When the farmer fell on hard times they sold their land to local money lenders or landlords, who allowed them to cultivate the land and give the landlord a portion of their harvest as payment as previously mentioned. Eventually, nearly all of the local citizens within the village lost their land to the money lenders and became indentured servants on the land they once owned. This was common throughout Asia and Indochina, which eventually led to the Cultural Revolution of the 1960's in China, where millions starved and the peasants rose-up against the land lords, whom they blamed for their plight. Mao Zedong wanted his cultural revolution to inspire a class revolution; however the people used it as an opportunity to take back their land from the landlords. Even though the farmer lost their land, it was only part of a much larger economic picture of failure.

Each village in rural Asia and in particular Indochina, were ruled by a local and regional governments. The village council owned all the land and distributed parcels to families to work and cultivate. If a family failed to work the land, the village council or elders would repossess the land and reassigned to another family. In exchange, they would give the village a portion of their harvest to the village cooperative (co-op). It would be distributed to families in the village who were elderly and unable to work their own land. If a family had difficulty planting or harvesting, the village council assigned families to help those who were unable to manage on their own, in exchange for portion of their harvest.

The system used in rural Asia and Indochina, was a form of socialism, but not communism. By definition it would be called a Traditional Economic System. The people owned the land in the village co-op or village collective and not a commune in which the government owned all of the land and the products that they produced. The Traditional Economic System was common in Thailand, Vietnam, Cambodia and Burma. It worked well on a small-scale where everyone was in the same social and economic class and status, but it would be much more difficult to administer on a larger national level, especially in a country as populated as China with its large urban population. The basic underlying principle of Marxism was to move the urban dwellers into the country and into agricultural communes so they could produce enough food to feed both the rural and urban population. It was also the reason communism couldn't possibly work in countries where a large percentage of the population lived in cities, because there weren't enough farmers to produce enough food for the entire population and much of the land was not suitable for agriculture. Eventually, communist countries had no other option but to gravitate toward a capitalist economic system.

China today is heading toward a new economic situation. They have placed much of their emphasis on manufacturing and industrialization that require the labor of young people that are paid low wages. As a result, young people are moving from the rural farms and into the cities for better pay. What remains in the rural villages are the older farmers who have little skill but agriculture. As

China industrializes, the need for more factory workers increases which leads to a decline in agricultural out-put which forces China to import and purchase more and more agricultural products abroad. China wanted to encourage more people to remain on the farms by issuing ID cards that designated those individuals who were born on farms and those who were born in the cities. For those who had ID cards from the city, it entitled them to free health care, retirement and government housing, while those from the rural agricultural villages, received no health care, retirement or housing allowances. It would take little imagination to see what the effects would be if it continues for the next 20 or 30 years. Should a person move from the rural village and work in a city, he would not receive the benefits that a coworker would receive if he were born in a city. This system guarantees that the poorer class of people will always remain poor and for the most part, the industrial blue-collar worker will always remain a blue-collar worker and middle class.

China today is working on a more equitable system to reverse the effects of an agricultural class and urban class of people in a communist country with a capitalist economic system. It will require fine tuning so that the rural farmer can keep pace monetarily with the urban worker and industrialization.

Most farmers and their families lived and died in their villages without ever traveling more than 50 miles from where they were born. They in fact had little idea about world of politics and who actually ran their government. Most Southeast Asia countries were Monarchs, in which the King or Queen ran the government with impunity. Their life became the village, their family, their friends and community. Every village had a market where the local farmer could sell their handicrafts, tools, fresh vegetables, fish and fruits. It was an agrarian society and based on a traditional efficient social system that has worked for thousands of years, and worked well under the circumstances.

The villagers had little education above a grade school level and worked in the fields planting and harvesting rice as soon as they were old enough to be of help. Their life revolved around survival and living from one day to the next and living a subsistence lifestyle. They never worried about the future, partly because they knew they couldn't change it and they knew no other way of life. In their eyes they thought the whole world lived like they did, one day to the next and living in a community social system.

The Ethnic Groups

There are about 50 to 60 ethnic tribal groups in China and Southeast Asia. Most migrated south from China along the border areas of Indochina, Thailand and Burma (Myanmar). The ethnic tribal groups lived in the mountainous regions of northern Thailand and Laos along the border of China and Vietnam. The Chinese persecuted ethnic group for their religious beliefs, especially during the cultural revolution of the 1960's when religious worship and basic freedoms were not tolerated. During that period in China, large numbers migrated south into the border regions of Thailand, Burma, Vietnam and Laos.

Most ethnic tribes settled in the mountainous regions of Southeast Asia because the land had little value for agricultural purposes, it forced them to cultivate poppies for opium as their primary cash crop. The Hmong (mong) is a sect of the Meo ethnic group that occupies most of the land that surrounds the Golden Triangle, which is an area about the size of Oregon (96,000 sq. miles), where the borders of Burma, Thailand and Laos meet. The Hmong were fierce and loyal fighters who fought alongside the French in the early 1950's during the French Indochina war against the communist. After the French pulled out of

Vietnam in 1954, they migrated into the remote regions of northern Laos and later were recruited to fight the Pathet Laos communist in Laos. Many Hmong became casualties of war during the French occupation and the American war in Laos while fighting the communist. After the war, and under the rule of the communist regime in Laos, entire villages were burned in retaliation for their support. Many migrated south into Thailand and some later resettled in America and Australia. Currently there are several thousand Hmong fighters in the mountains of Laos, who are still operating as guerilla fighters against the communist Laos Regime. (This will be discussed in detail in Chapter 7)

Communist Manifesto

Karl Marx wrote the Communist Manifesto in 1848. It became Lenin's inspiration for the Russian revolution of 1917. Marx's Manifesto maintained that a society should be classless, where there are no upper, middle or lower class of people. The entire population would be one single class run by 200 loyal communist members that were elected every five years to the Central Committee. The Politburo is a 7 to 9 member committee that runs the daily operation of the communist government. The General Secretary, also called the Chairman, is head of the Politburo. Under the theory of Marxism, communism could only work if the country was both an advanced industrial nation and an agrarian society, in other words, a uniform mix of both classes. This is an important element in Marx's Manifesto, because Marx wasn't certain if his theoretical hypothesis would actually work. His theory depended on a large middle class leading the revolution against the Bourgeois, and not the lower class. His system required 4 phases to complete until total utopia could be obtained:

1. Revolution must take place to destroy the existing government and system. This meant that all non-communist believers would be purged from the system.

2. The leader selected is a dictator capable of controlling the proletariat (working class).

3. Collectivization of property and personal wealth would be seized.

4. The government would control all forms of production, manufacturing and agriculture. Only the lower working class people would exists within the system. [26]

For the system to operate as Karl Marx intended, the Government would need to control all elements of banking, education, labor and industry in the country. In addition they would needed to control transportation, communications, factories, farms and land. In Short, the government would own everything except food and clothing and a few personal items for which they would receive a small monthly stipend from the government for personal items. This is where the lines between socialism and communism becomes blurred and in some cases merge. The two systems have different ideologies but can appear similar from outside appearances. Fascism is a dictatorial socialism with a single party dictator who allows privately owned businesses under strict oversight by the government. Smaller businesses of lesser importance were owned by the state, some were also own by the people.

It's possible that over time, communism, socialism and democracy could gradually morph into something entirely different from the economic and political system we are familiar with today. Communist states could move toward socialism and drift toward a form of democracy, but only if they abolish the Politburo and the Central

Committee like the Soviet Union did. However, America could gravitate toward a Plutocracy or even socialism similar to Sweden. The wealthy and corporate America could dictate policy to the government and establish a foreign policy that would favor corporate business interest. Government officials could be former CEO's in business and banking. It is almost inevitable that the United States will gradually shift toward a Plutocracy while Communist States could shift toward a mild form of socialism with a capitalist economic system. Politics is like water, it eventually seeks its own level, somewhere in the middle.

In regards to communism, Karl Marx died before he could prove and test his theory, in fact, even today it has never been tested in the same context he envisioned, but Vladimir Lenin in 1917 would test a modified version of Marx's theory.

Lenin's vision of Communism followed closely to Marxism, but he knew he couldn't convince the upper and middle class to join his communist cause, partly because his goal was to eliminate upper and middle classes. He targeted mostly the poor and working class to rise up against the Bourgeois. Russia in 1917, was one of the poorest countries in Europe, and had little industrialization, so it was easy for Lenin to convince the people to rise up against the Czar and the Bourgeois, who controlled most of the power and wealth in the country. Joseph Stalin was active in the 1917 communist revolution when the Bolsheviks seized control of the Russian Government under the leadership of Lenin. He established a seven member Politburo and a Central Committee of about 200 party loyalists. As one of the original revolutionaries in 1922, Stalin was appointed General Secretary of the seven members Politburo.

The General Secretary had authority to appoint only those who were loyal to himself and not necessarily loyal to the party. He purposely excluded members to party meetings who he felt did not agree with his ideology on how the government should be run. When Lenin died in 1924, it wasn't long before Stalin became Chairman of the Communist Party.

Mao Zedong's Vision of Marxism

Mao Zedong attempted to adapt the Marxist communist Manifesto to Lenin's version of communism. Mao advocated change through revolution. Under Mao's brand of communism, the poor people could remove members of the communist committee if any member strayed from the Marxism through take-over and revolution. This is what started the cultural revolution of the 1960's under Mao's encouragement of change by revolution. The Central Communist Committee became dominated by radical Marxist within the Central Committee who were deemed disloyal to Mao's vision of Marxism. Members were purged, exiled or sent to labor camps. Over time, more than 1 ½ million became victims of the purge, while another one million perished in prisons, starvation and torture as a result of the Revolution. Overzealous Red Guards, whom Mao encouraged, carried-out the cleansing of all non-believers in his Maoist communist agenda. (This will be discussed in detail in Chapter 3).

Mao Zedong's austere and cult personality was similar to Hitler, Mussolini, and Kim Il-Sung. The one thing that made their rise to power easy was that each country was facing difficult economic times, and propaganda could be used to convince citizens that classes of people were the cause of their misery and plight. In the 20th Century, propaganda became an art, and many cult leaders were able to persuade the public that change was needed through revolution.

Propaganda was often the tool used to discredit political opponents and turn popular opinion against them. Mao perfected this technique and used it against those he disliked. In 1960 the Politburo was leaning toward a capitalist market economy. He called those who wanted both a communist system and a capitalist economy, "Capitalist Roaders", in which Mao despised. He gave speeches and wanted the people to rise-up and revolt against those in government who wanted change. **[Footnote 1]**

The key to success in any government is a large and healthy middle and working class. The term "Bourgeois", means the middle and upper class who were the owners of land and developed the means of manufacturing products. [26] The middle class were not poor but not rich either. They obtained a modest education and were most often blue-collar workers who were the back-bone of the industrialized economy. The middle class were much more tolerant of the failures of government and seldom revolted over inequities, whereas the poor believed revolution was the only means for change.

Without the middle class, there would only be a two class system; Rich and Poor. The rich will most always take advantage of the poor because of their station in life, and the poor had little political standing that could be easily manipulated. It would eventually create resentment between the two divisions in society. In third world countries, the poor outnumber the rich by 9 to 1. This is how the revolutionaries were able to establish a foot hold, while appealing to the vast number of poor people to rise up against the affluent to get their slice of the economic pie.

Under the Marxist theory, Marx envisioned that the middle class would rise-up and revolt against the

Bourgeois (affluent), who controlled industry, agriculture and businesses.

Under Leninism, Stalinism and Maoism, it was the poor and lower middle class that revolted against the establishment, which was contrary to the theory espoused by Karl Marx, where the middle class would rise up against the elite.

In Russia in the early 1900's, as many as 80% of the people were poor and lower working class, while less than 20% were middle class and upper class. This was one of the flaws in Karl Marx's theory. Today, in third world countries, about 71 of the population are poor working class and 13 % are middle class. In contrast, to the United States, 26% are poor and lower working class while 63% are middle class and only 10% are upper or wealthy class. So in general, most countries turn to violence and revolt when they feel there is an inequity and wide disparity between classes, and where their concerns are not being addressed by the government, or caused by government.

Even though this may seem like a simplistic explanation of a complicated issue of why people revolt and demand change, but in reality, it is not complicated, it is just people fed up with the inequities of a class system. It makes little sense to analyze it any more than that.

Stalin's Rise to Power

Joseph Stalin was born in Gori, Georgia in 1878. He was only 5 foot 4 inches tall, with thick black hair and a thick black mustache and hazel eyes. He had a pocked marked face as a result of chicken pox when he was young. When he was twelve years old, he was involved in a horse carriage accident that permanently injured his left arm. After several surgeries, his left arm was shorter than his right arm, so in all of his photos he held his left arm to his side as if to hide it from view.

Stalin trusted no one, and gradually exterminated his closest confidants and allies as a result of his paranoia. He became indifferent toward human life and once told an army commander that they should clear mine fields by marching troops over them rather than using a mine sweepers, because it was much faster and less expensive.

Stalin would not allow his guards into his bedroom under any circumstances, "even if he were dying" as he told his guards. To test his guard's loyalty, one day while in his bedroom he began to scream and yell as if injured. When one of his body guards opened the door to see if he was alright, he had him arrested and executed for failing to follow orders. In 1953, Stalin had a Paralyzing seizure and fell to the floor, gasping loudly trying to summon help. He lay on the floor for four hours, until Peter Lozgachev, Deputy Commandant, arrived and found him semi-conscious. When Lozgachev, summoned the guards to help him, they refused to enter his bedroom to aid, but thought it was another one of Stalin's loyalty test. Stalin died one week later at the age of 75.

Stalin's Great Purge

In 1932, rumors were being circulated among party members criticizing Stalin's policies. Some members wanted Stalin's long time arch-enemy, Leon Trotsky, to be re-instated into the party. When the issue came before the Politburo for a vote, Stalin wanted the dissenters arrested and executed. His longtime friend and confidant, Sergey Kirov, was head of the Leningrad Communist Party and argued against Stalin's recommendation in front of the Politburo, and during a vote the majority sided with Kirov. This small and insignificant footnote in history will change the history of the Soviet Union and how people will remember him. Sergey Kirov was a popular party member in both the Communist Central Committee and among the people. Because of Kirov's popularity, Stalin felt he had to keep a close eye on Kirov else his power could be compromised or undermined.

In 1934, Kirov wanted to release political prisoners who opposed Stalin's policy on collective farms and industrialization policy. Once again Stalin and Kirov faced-off and argued their points in front of the Politburo and Kirov won the majority vote. Stalin being jealous of Kirov and resented the fact that his policies were being overruled consistently by his closest friend, he formulated a plan. [38]

Stalin and Kirov both went on holiday together in the summer of 1934, which offered Stalin a great opportunity for him to persuade Kirov to leave Leningrad and move to Moscow and be apart of his inner circle, but Kirov declined the offer. At that point, he knew he had eliminated Kirov; else his authority and position within the party would deteriorate even further as his charismatic friend could eventually take Stalin's position as Party Chairman and leader of Russia.

On December 1, 1934, Sergey Kirov was assassinated by a party member named Leonid Nikolayev. Although Nikolayev may not have been known by Stalin, it was strongly suspected that Stalin was involved and ordered the execution. With the assassination of Kirov, it was a perfect opportunity for Stalin to purge his potential rivals in the Politburo and the Central Party under the auspices of hunting down the conspirators to Kirov's death.

As a result of Kirov's assignation, Stalin executed party members whom he felt had a motive to kill Kirov. Hundreds of prisoners from Leningrad whom Stalin felt was disloyal became victims of mass executions. The reign of terror continued within the Central Committee until 93 of the 139 committee members became victims of his purge. Of the 1.9 million communist party members in the Soviet Union, more than 800,000 fell under Stalin's reign of terror. Public trials were held in which more than a dozen party members who confessed to being involved in the assassination (perhaps under torture and false confessions which is common with dictators), accused Trotsky as the ring leader of the plot. Some claim that Stalin himself was a target of the assassination. Trotsky had long since exiled himself to Mexico years before, however, several years later, he was found dead in his apartment of an apparent blow to the back of his head with a pick axe, obviously not from suicide. [38]

In June of 1937, eight top Soviet Army commanders were accused of conspiring with the Germans. A mock trial found all eight guilty and all eight were executed. Over the course of the summer, 30,000 soldiers also became victims. During the course of Stalin's purge, half of the Soviet military officers met their death for allegedly conspiring to overthrow Stalin. One theory was that the Nazi's planted the information so that Stalin would think that his military commanders conspired with the Germans to overthrow him. [38] This was perhaps not the case however, but Stalin didn't need an excuse to rid his generals whom he thought was capable of planning a coup d'état at some point in time.

Chapter 2

Japan's Quest for Expansion

Much of the hate and resentment between Japan, China, Korea and Russia began as early as1894, during the first Sino-Japanese War of 1895 and the Russo-Japanese War of 1904. Most were ruled by Monarchs in which pride and obstinacy was their virtue. Each were suspicious of each other which resulted in a growing resentment and distrust towards each other.

One single ruler would invade another country over the slightest trivial event; such was the case in the Russo-Japanese War of 1894, which started over the fear of Russia leasing an ice free port from China. Japan thought Russia was intending to expand its influence into Asia and would become a threat to Japan's expansionist plans.

The Emperor Mutsuhito, also known as Meiji, ruled Japan from 1867 to 1912. Some say he brought Japan out of the dark ages in which Japan emerged as major world power. Hirohito, ruled Japan from 1926 until Japan's defeat in World War II in 1945. After the war, Japan became a Constitutional Monarch and Hirohito ruled until his death in 1989. His son Akihito became Emperor.

China was ruled by the Qing Dynasty until the Nationalist took over in February of 1912, and Puyi, "the last Emperor", being of minor age, was forced to abdicate his throne. He would later be called upon by the Japanese to become a puppet ruler of Manchuria, which Japan would later rename "Manchukuo".

There were two Sino-Japanese wars; the First occurred in 1894 that lasted until 1895, and the Second from 1937 to 1945, which spilled over into World War II, and ended with the surrender of Japan in 1945. The first Sino-Japanese war started over the control of Korea and the Korean Peninsula in which the Japanese refused to pull-out Korea as mutually agreed upon by the Chinese-Russian Li-ito Convention of 1885, also known as the Tientsin Conventions.

Russo-Japanese War

Russia needed an ice-free port in the Far East for its naval fleet, because Vladivostok's port in Siberia was only ice–free during the short summer months. Japan's growing influence and the taste for expansion worried Nicholas II of Russia. The naval port of Port Arthur on the Liaodong Peninsula in China was a year-round port and was leased to Russia in 1898, with an option to renew for another 25 years. Once the lease agreement was signed, Russia began to build a railroad from Port Arthur to Manchuria and road into northern Korea. A dispute developed between Japan and Russia over the naval fleet stationed at Port Arthur. Through a series of negotiations between Japan and Czar Nicholas II failed to materialize. Japan made an offer to Russia giving it control of Manchuria in exchange for Japan's occupation of Korea. Russia refused the offer and demanded a portion of the Korean Peninsula above the 38th parallel, as a buffer zone between Japan. After repeated negotiations over the next two year, both parties failed to reach a compromise.

On February 8, 1904, just 3 hours before the declaration of war was received by the Russian government, the Japanese Imperial Navy attacked Russia's Naval Fleet at Port Arthur for the purpose of neutralizing Russia's Far East fleet in port. Czar Nicholas II was stunned belated to learn that Japan violated the rules of war and declared war on Japan eight days later. The Qing Empire in China took sides with Japan and offered military aid, but Japan refused. This was another switch in diplomacy, since China leased Port Arthur to Russia in 1898 and now switched loyalties. **[Footnote 2]**

Even though Admiral Togo's attack was not decisive, it allowed the Japanese time to land troops near Incheon, Korea and annex most of the Korean Peninsula. Port Arthur in China was under siege and was being blockaded by the Japanese war ships, so that Russian ships couldn't go in or out of the harbor to rally an effective attack against the Japanese Naval forces.

Over the next year, Japan and Russia engaged in numerous naval and ground battles, where Japan in an effort to gained the upper hand, forced Russia to sue for peace. In September of 1905, President Theodore Roosevelt mediated the Treaty of Portsmouth in New Hampshire, between Japan and Russia, where Japan would annex Korea and agree to evacuate Manchuria. In addition, Russia signed over its 25 year lease of Port Arthur and the Sakhalin Islands to Japan. In total, more than 47,000 Japanese and 52,000 Russians were killed in the war. [39] [40]

The defeat of Russia in the Russo-Japanese War was viewed by the Chinese nationalist and the Qing Dynasty as a war between Asia and Europe. The Empress Dowager Cixi and her nephew Emperor Guangxu were having problems with the "Boxer's" in China, who were rioting and murdering foreigners and demanding that all foreigners leave China. As a protective measure, each country built military garrisons to protect their expatriates and land holdings, such as Macau and Hong Kong and Shanghai. Foreign gun boats were common along the Yangtze River, trolling the river in a show of force that represented every nation who had a vested interest in China.

The Empress felt that Europeans were foreign invaders who were taking advantage of Asia and giving little or nothing in return. She didn't have the military strength to drive the invaders out, so they were coerced into making compromises which were not necessarily in their best interest. As a result, Britain took control of Hong Kong and the Portuguese protectorate of Macau. This is perhaps the primary reason why China switched loyalties when the war started, but they overlooked Japan's ulterior motives for war.

Japan had a different motive for wanting Russia out of Asian. The defeat of Russia demonstrated to the world that Japan had become a world naval power with mobility throughout Asia, capable of taking on European naval powers in battle, should it become necessary. Japan tested its military strength for the purpose of dominating Asia for its natural resources, which Japan needed to industrialize and become a world industrial power. For Japan, it gave a sense of pride knowing they were able to expand their sphere of influence throughout Asia. There were two different motives, and the theory will be tested in the second Sino-Japanese War when Japan once again, when Japan invades Manchuria and China in 1931. This time China feels the full wrath of the Japanese Imperial Army, which had been building up for nearly thirty-five years.

When Japan annexed Korea in 1910, Emperor Gwangmu of Korea was ordered to abdicate his throne; however he refused and instead appointed his son, Yunghui to succeed him. Emperor Yunghui was also forced to abdicate and would become the last Emperor of Korea. Japan would rule Korea for the next 35 years.

Historians agree that there were two reasons why Japan invaded Manchuria in 1931; the first being the need for raw natural resources for continued industrialization and the desire to have all of Asia under a single emperor, preferably by the Japanese emperor, Hirohito.

Chapter 3

The Sino-Japanese War

As briefly mentioned in chapter 2, there were two Sino-Japanese Wars. The first Sino-Japanese war occurred between 1894 and 1895, which began as a result of Japan seizing Korea, Formosa and some islands in the South China Sea.

The second Sino-Japanese war began in 1937, however, hostilities began as early as 1928, between China and Japan with the invasion of Manchuria in 1931. Little historical attention has been given to the War, partly because it was overshadowed by the Great Depression of 1929, and America's declared neutrality and later World War II in 1941. European Allies; Britain and France, were more concerned about Hitler's invasion of Austria and Poland, which was more of a threat than the events in Asia. America declared its neutrality shortly after World War I, but offered a lend lease agreement with England and Russia for materials and weapons to counter Hitler's quest for new territory in Europe.

America had no territorial claims in China other than supporting Chiang-Kai-Shek, who was in firm control of much of Central China while fighting Mao's Communist guerrillas for control of China. In 1931, the second Sino-Japanese war started as a result of a long standing Japanese Imperialist policy of expansion under Emperor Hirohito. Japan needed the raw materials for industrialization, food and conscripted labor to satisfy its goals of expansion and domination. Korea and Manchuria, provided the conscripted labor, but Korea had little natural resources of its own. They needed oil, timber, iron, rubber and tin, desperately. In 1931, Japan invaded Manchuria with a small army for the purpose of seizing control and establishing a mainland base near the border of Manchuria and Northern China. They already controlled the Korean Peninsula from the first Sino-Japanese war and the Russo-Japanese War of 1905, so they orchestrated several small localized engagements deep into Manchuria and along the Chinese and Siberian borders.

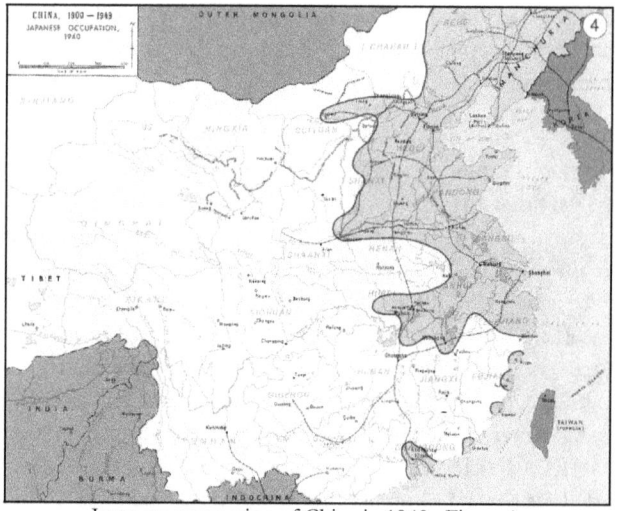

Japanese occupation of China in 1940. Figure 1a

In 1932, Japan established the puppet state called Manchukuo, also known as Manchuria and named Puyi, the last surviving Emperor of China as ruler, albeit under Japanese over-sight. China had already engaged in a civil war between Chiang Kai-Shek's Nationalist Army and Mao Zedong's Communist Revolutionaries when Japan invaded Manchuria. Japan's goal was to keep both armies separated and occupied so both Chinese Armies couldn't amass a unified defense against the Japanese invasion force. This would change when the Japanese advanced further south toward the Great Wall in an effort to establish a buffer zone around key military strong holds near China's northern border. To avoid war, Chiang-Kai-Shek was hesitant to intervene, since much of Northern China was in the control of war lords and a small nationalist Army sent to help fight Japan. The League of Nations investigated Japan's invasion of Manchuria and condemned Japan for its incursion, which prompted Japan to withdraw as a member of the League of Nations.

Once occupying Manchuria they advanced near Beijing and controlled most of the Northern Provinces and coastal provinces in China. Conflicts continued between the Japanese and local war lords and the nationalist over the next 5 years with twenty-two engagements and skirmishes for control of Northern China. In July of 1937, Chinese and Japanese troops engaged in a skirmish near Beijing at the Marco Polo Bridge, which escalated into a full scale Battle and invasion by the Japanese military, who stormed the city of Beijing and the Port of Tianjing. Chiang Kai-shek and his Kuomintang (KMT) Nationalist Army engaged the Japanese in August of 1937 for control of Shanghai which resulted in a win for the Japanese army, however at a terrible casualty loss to the Japanese with more than a 50% their aircraft destroyed. On December 5, 1937, Hirohito decided to send his son, Prince Asaka, to Command the Japanese troops. Asaka ordered the army to advance toward the KMT's Capital of Nanking and destroy it. **[Footnote 3]** The battle for Nanking was not easy, since it was a walled city and well fortified, however it fell to the Japanese in only four days, but Chiang Kai-Shek's army had pulled out of Nanking nine days earlier.

The Nanking Massacre

Lieutenant Generals Kesago Nakajima and Heisuke Yanagawa informed Asaka when he arrived from Tokyo, that they had surrounded 300,000 Chinese troops in Nanking. In retrospect, this may have been an over exaggeration, it was perhaps about 60,000 troops. [Footnote 4]

On December 9th, the Japanese arrived at the walled city and demanded that Chiang Kai-shek's KMT Army surrender within 24 hours. Chiang Kai-shek, however, had already fled the city and left General Tang Sheng-chi with a small military contingent of about 60,000 troops to hold off the Japanese while Chiang Kai-shek's army could make a safe retreat. Japanese General Iwane Matsui was responsible for the invasion force in the city.

On December 12, 1937, Matsui ordered heavy artillery and air bombardment of Nanking. The entire city was in a state of chaos as all of the gates in and out of the city were blocked by Japanese soldiers.

As Chinese troops fled the city, they were shot. The following day, the Japanese troops entered the city and established a Safety Zone for foreigners and diplomats' who were relocated within a 4 kilometer square area within the walled city. The purpose of the Safety Zone was to protect the foreign expatriates from the injury.

The foreigners organized their own International Committee headed by an American named John Rabe. The Japanese made it clear to all expatriates in the Safety Zone, that if they ventured out of the Zone for any reason, they were not responsible for their safety.

The Japanese secured the city, on December 13, 1937; Hirohito gave a directive concerning the Geneva Conventions of 1929, which took effect in June of 1931, in which he stated that the treatment of Chinese prisoners would not be adhered to by Japan. He advised them not to use the term "prisoner of war" when referring to the captured Chinese. [41]

Japanese soldiers cheer as they took the walled city of Nanking in December of 1937   Fig. 1

The purpose of the directive was to inform the Japanese field commanders that any Chinese who were captured need not go to a prisoner of war camp or be treated as prisoners of war. Only two countries did not sign the Geneva Convention of 1929, Japan and Russia.

The Commanders were given indirect orders to execute the Chinese rather than placing them in camps. The events that occurred would precipitate into the massacre of Nanjing. This single act in Nanjing turned world opinion against Japan and labeled them as barbarous invaders similar to Genghis Khan, however, even Genghis Khan established a policy of avoiding the torture and mutilation of prisoners when captured.   America capitalized on Japan's barbarous acts as propaganda campaigns against Japan as being ruthless barbarians, which helped turn American's opinion against the Japanese and unit American's against a common enemy.

Once Nanjing fell, the Japanese searched for KMT soldiers who had hidden in the city and shed their uniforms for peasant clothing. In the end, 57,000 surrendered, many were not military, which made little difference, since they were given instructions from Hirohito not to take any prisoners, civilian or military.

They escorted the prisoners to the edge of the bank on the Yangtze River and bound them together, then shot them. A Japanese soldier tied the captives together; and when he shot the first captive, the rest would plummet over the bank and into the murky river and drown. The Japanese marched 1,300 Chinese soldiers and civilians in front of the Taiping Gate and executed them. American journalists and businessmen in Nanjing witnessed much of the massacre and later reported the atrocities to newspapers in America and around the world.

In addition to the execution of Chinese soldiers, the Japanese raped and then executed 20,000 women. Many victims were mutilated after being raped, according to the International Military Tribunal for the Far East. [42] To complicate the situation further, the "Panay Incident" occurred in Nanjing during the Japanese invasion of Nanking. The United States had a naval gun boat called the "Panay" on the Yangtze River, along with several oil tankers owned by Standard Oil Company.

The purpose of the gun boat was to protect Americans and American business interests during the civil war at the time. On December 12, 1937, Japanese fighters and bombers attacked the ships and sank them. Even though they had 3 American flags in open display, the Japanese maintained they did not see the flags and thought they were Chinese.

Japan apologized for the sinking of the ships and paid reparations, but it is widely believed that the attack was intentional.

Japanese preparing to execute two Chinese Soldier, fig. 2

With the fall of Beijing, Shanghai and Nanking; Japan occupied much of the North, northern coastal regions and the central plains along the Yangtze River. But much of the western interior remained under the control of the Communist Revolutionaries and the Nationalist Army of Chiang Kai-Shek. Even though Japan continued to import more troops numbering as many as 900,000, they were cautious, if not hesitant to advance into China's interior, and remained mostly in the larger cities. Chiang entered talks with Mao to join forces to drive the Japanese out of China and implemented the strategy of "trading space for time" which delayed Japanese advancement in the West and South. The Chinese strategy was to drag-out the war as long as possible while stalling while halting any further advancement into the interior, thus allowing them to build a sizeable military and regroup. By June of 1939, the joint Chinese army had 2.6 million regular soldiers, excluding the war lords and local village militia.

Kill all, Loot all, Burn all Policy

In the Japanese controlled cities in the east, constant sabotage of the railroads and coal mines were being conducted underground resistance forces, which were frustrating the Japanese.   Even the harbors and docks became targets for the underground.   These attacks prompted the Japanese to issue the order, "kill all, loot all, burn all". As the Japanese advance to the west stalled by late 1939 and early 1940, conflict between the Communist Party of China (CPC) and the KMT rekindle again, with numerous confrontations between the two armies. The KMT under Chiang Kai-Shek was now fighting two armies; the Communist and the Japanese.   Chiang's strategy against the CPC was to form a blockade and confine the communist within the rural areas, which allowed Mao time to organize and indoctrinate and reform rural communities into the communist principals and ideals. In the end, the CPC grew in size while the KMT slowly decreased in size by attrition, as a result of fighting the Japanese. The CPC elected to use guerilla warfare of hit and run and as a result, they had one-third the casualties as the KMT. This strategy was not orchestrated by accident, it was well planned by Mao to have the Nationalist army fight the Japanese while the CPC would only engage in guerrilla warfare of hit and run only when necessary for defense. The Japanese wasn't concerned about taking land, but rather the cities, which was the center of government. Mao had in his favor, knowledge of rural China. He was aware that 60% of the population lived in rural China as farmers and were easy victims for reform and a promise of a better life.

While Chiang Kai-Shek battled the Japanese, Mao aggressively recruited rural farmers to his cause. He had taken refuge in western China, far from the battle front, which was being fought between the Nationalist and the Japanese. [Footnote 5]   It is important to note that China today does not acknowledge the great accomplishments and sacrifice of the Nationalist Army in fighting the Japanese, but rather has selectively given credit to Mao Zedong's Communist guerrillas as the liberators of China from the Japanese which was not the case. It was all part of a scheme to build-up communism and denounce the merits of the nationalist and their role in eventually defeating the Japanese occupation.

Japan establishes Puppet Governments in China

Japan was having difficulty maintaining order in the cities, especially the constant sabotage of military and supply facilities by the Chinese underground, which was frustrating the Japanese.   They decided to install local Chinese mayors and former leaders in key positions in puppet Chinese government by late 1938.   Even though most decisions were decided by the Japanese command, there were always opportunist who relished the opportunity of being on the winning side and having power and authority, regardless who side they were on.

One such person was Wang Jing Wei, who was one of the original Sun Yat-sen's leaders and founders of the Kuomintang (KMT) army. After Sun Yat-sen's death in 1925, Chiang Kai-Shek would take control of the Nationalist KMT for which Wang Jingwei felt he was entitled and next in line.   They became bitter rivals, but Wang Jing Wei's popularity forced Chiang Kai-Shek to consider him as Prime Minister, even though they were in constant conflict with each other's policies.

After a tumultuous period between the two, in late 1938, Wang Jing Wei would resign from the KMT and support the Japanese as a retaliatory measure against Chiang and the KMT party. Japan was quick to appoint him as Head of State for the Reorganized National Government of China in Nanking, even though his authority extended only to territories under Japanese occupation. He established relations with the German Nazis and Italian fascist and continued that relationship during the period he was Head of State for the Japanese.

The Chinese people considered all puppet officials as traitors and a great deal of resentment developed between the populous and the Chinese installed government which only fueled more sabotage and assassinations. Jing Wei assumed that after the war, he would be the Head of State for China, as long as Japan wins the war, but by 1943, it was becoming obvious that the tide of war was turning against Japan. There were assignation attempts on his life and at one point he returned to Japan for an operation from an assassins bullet and died in Tokyo in 1944. Had he lived he would have surely been hung as a traitor and a collaborator with the enemy.

As if things couldn't get worse for China; the Soviet Union invades China's Xingjiang Province in 1937. General Ma Hushan who was loyal to the KMT, was an ethnic Muslim Hui who fought the Soviets, Japanese and the communist. Chiang Kai-Shek sent General Ma Buqing north with 30,000 troops to halt the advancement of the Soviets and reclaim the Xingjiang Province. Much of the outer reaches of China were being fought by ethnic Hui and Chinese Muslims who were decisive in defeating the Soviets and holding key positions and corridors.

The Japanese became frustrated with the Hui Muslims and implemented the "Killing Policy" in 1941. More than 220 mosques were destroyed and entire villages were burned and forced Hui women into sex slavery or comfort women. In Manchuria, Korean and Japanese women were also used as comfort women for the Japanese and Manchurian Army, however, many would marry Chinese and Manchurian men and were not allowed back into Korea or Japan after the war.

After America entered the War in 1941, and its neutrality vacated, the US supplied the Chinese troops with tanks, trucks, guns and artillery to fight the Japanese, which by 1943 pushed the Japanese East and toward the coast of China, confining them to a much smaller area. Many Japanese troops in Manchuria and China were ordered to return to Japan for a possible invasion by the allied forces of mainland Japan. They needed at least 1 million soldiers to defend the homeland. and China was the only viable option Japan had. In doing so, it would leave only 450,000 Japanese to defend China against Chiang Kai-Shek and Mao's 2.5 million troops. It would ultimately be the end of Japan's control over China and Indo-China. Chiang Kai-Shek would later administer the surrender of the Japan in China and Vietnam in 1945, only to be defeated by Mao Zedong's communist forces in China in 1948.

Chapter 4

World War II in Asia

The bombing of Pearl Harbor in 1941 was the result of a United States embargo of oil and steel to Japan over the invasion of China and Manchuria. When negotiations failed between Japan and the United States, war was declared between the two countries, followed by Germany as part of the Axis powers with Japan and Italy.

Stalin was betrayed by Hitler in World War II when in August of 1939, both entered a non-aggression agreement called the Molotov-Ribbentrop Pact, where both would invade Poland and divide Poland between them. This Pact was exactly what Hitler needed to keep from having to fight a war on two fronts. Hitler was certain that if he invaded Poland, Britain and France would declare war on Germany and he needed some form of assurance from Russian that Stalin would not join the Allied Forces and attack Germany from the east. As a result of the invasion of Poland, France and Britain did declare war on Germany as he predicted, however Hitler met his match when he aligned himself with Stalin, because soon after invading Poland, Stalin immediately invaded Finland and shortly after, the Baltic States and Romania. Hitler had to stop Stalin's aggression into Baltic States because he needed the oil fields in Romania for himself. Hitler then implemented "Operation Barbarossa", which was a plan to invade the Soviet Union in June of 1941.

Stalin was completely taken off guard by the German invasion, so much so, that Stalin locked himself in his country estate for 3 weeks while Hitler's Army raced across the Ukraine. His commanders pleaded with him to take charge before it was too late. It was at this point in history, when Stalin would never trust another person again, and became indifferent towards his troops. When he did emerge, he took charge of the Soviet Army and successfully pushed the Germans out of Russia, but at a cost of 4 million of his own troops. When his son was captured by the Nazi's, the German's wanted to trade his son for two German generals that had been capture by the Russians. Stalin sent a reply to Berlin, "I don't trade soldiers for generals". When his son heard the reply from Stalin, he threw himself into an electrified fence in a POW camp and killed himself.

During Operation Barbarossa, the Soviet army advanced toward the German battle lines in two fronts, the first being the main battle front and the second followed a quarter mile behind. The purpose of these two battle positions wasn't a military strategy, but rather a technique to keep the main advancing Soviet force from retreating during battle. Should the main force retreat, the second front would fire upon the retreating force. Needless to say, most of the Soviet casualties during the war were at the hands of their very own comrades.

Should a Russian Soldier be captured by the Germans' during combat and sent to a prisoner of war camp for the duration of the war, after the war Stalin would send the Russian prisoners to a Siberian Gulag work camp. Stalin's rationale was; the prisoner's must have been cowards to get caught and secondly, deserved to be sent back to prison in the Soviet Union.

There were seldom enough guns and ammunition to go around, so soldiers would go into battle in groups of two's, so if one were killed, the other would get his rifle and ammunition and continue the fight. Millions of Soviet troops were killed during Barbarossa, most as a result of a severe shortage of military arms and equipment and poor leadership.

Desertion was common in the Russian military, yet the option of retreat or desertion was not tolerated. None the less, there continued to be widespread desertion in the Soviet Army.

Operation Barbarossa, The German invasion of Minsk, Russia
1941   Fig. 5

President Roosevelt and Truman accepted Stalin back into the Allied alliance toward the end of World War II, which was perhaps a big mistake, but Roosevelt felt his alliance maybe need during an imminent invasion of mainland Japan. America's role in the early stage of Operation Barbarossa began in 1941 with a lend lease agreement between Stalin and Roosevelt.   America provided food, weapons, airplanes, vehicles and clothing for the Soviet Army to fight the Germans. Even though the Soviets had the greatest casualty rate of World War II, they were able to push the German military machine back to Berlin by 1945.

Stalin's goal was to secure as much territory as possible. He needed Korea and Indochina as part of his sphere of influence and to protect his "back door" against a Chinese or Japanese invasion, whom he felt both were a growing threat. After World War II, Stalin began to create a satellite communist network of communist states in Asia and Eastern Europe after the War.

Most of the Asian countries had to establish their own form of government after their independence from European colonization. The French gave-up independence to Indochina, the British to Burma, India and Malaysia, and the Netherlands to Indonesia. Japan relinquished Korea and Formosa and America gave independence to the Philippines.

Unit 731, the Asian holocaust

Perhaps one of the best kept secrets of World War II was Japan's involvement in human and chemical warfare experiments. During the war, America had no idea that special Japanese research units were conducting human medical experiments on Chinese, Russians and captured troops.

In 1932, General Shiro Ishii and the Japanese Chief Medical Officer, Sadao Araki were appointed to command the Army Epidemic Prevention Research Laboratory near the town of Pingfang, Harbin province in Northern China. The name of the facility was later changed to the Epidemic Prevention and Water Purification Department of the Kwantung Army. In reality, it started out as a biological and Chemical warfare research facility, but after the Sino-Japanese War of 1937, it included within its curriculum, human medical experimentation on a scale unimaginable, even by Nazi standards. It was the most egregious acts of human torture and crimes against humanity ever. Unit 731 wasn't the only Unit that was conducting experiments on humans and biological and chemical warfare against civilians; Unit 100 and Unit 1644 were also affiliated research units in China and Manchuria that were also performing medical experimentation.

After the Japanese surrender in August of 1945, allied forces found as many as five facilities and labs in Japan, China, Philippines and Manchuria. After the bombing of Hiroshima, the Japanese notified Washington that 8 American prisoners of war were killed in Hiroshima Castle as a result of the Atomic bomb blast. When the bodies were examined by an American pathologist, they found that the Japanese had performed human medical experiments on them and they died as a result of experiments, weeks before August 6, 1945 bombing. [54]

Most of the human experiments were conducted on Chinese, Koreans, Mongolians, Russian, mentally ill patients, subversives and pregnant women. Unit 731 and its affiliated units created separate departments whose job was to find and transport potential victims to the facility so there could be an endless supply of victims. Local police also cooperated by rounding-up poor and homeless, thieves and gypsies and labeled them "Special Delivery", which was understood to mean, "Transport to Unit 731". With such an active program, it required thousands of victims; in fact, one report said that 10,000 victims per year were needed to keep Unit 731 and its affiliate units in operation. [59]

In the Shinjuku District of Tokyo, Unit 731 operated a medical school and research facility in which medical students could operate on live humans as a teaching aid. In 2006, a retired nurse at the facility told government officials that she helped bury bodies and body parts on medical school grounds after Japan's surrender, so that the American's wouldn't find them. [59]

After the war it was discovered that medical experiments were conducted on captured Allied troops, mostly aviators and crew members. Of course, the medical experiments on Allied troops had to have a fatal result, else once the war was over, perpetrators would certainly be held accountable. The exact number of deaths are not known, but based on the data given to America after the war; it is believed that more than 3,000 died as a result of medical experiments in Unit 731, and perhaps another 9,000 from other Units. It has been estimated that as many as 1 million were subjected to Germ and Chemical warfare experiments as well. Mass graves were recently found where an estimated 250,000 bodies were buried, which authorities believed to be part of Unit 731 chemical warfare experiments. [57]

Most of those who were in prisons in Japan were listed as missing in action; obviously many may have been victims of human experiments or death by starvation and torture. Much of the data acquired during the experiments were shared with Germany, since both were members of the Axis powers. The project code name was "Maruta" which meant "Logs" in Japan. To the local people, the Japanese told them that Unit 731 facility in China was a Lumber mill, and jokingly the staff would ask, "how many logs fell today?" meaning how many were killed in the course of research that day. [45]

Of all the experiments conducted perhaps the most morbid was vivisections, which involved cutting into and dissecting a living body and removing body parts while the victim was still alive, and in most cases, without anesthesia. Researchers removed, liver, heart, lungs, limbs, brain and stomachs of victims to see how long they could survive without specific organs. They even amputated arms and legs and re-attached them to the other side of the body, of course all this was done without anesthesia, because the medical staff thought it may taint the research results.

They conducted experiments to see how long people could survive in cold water and survive in subzero temperatures. Almost all, who involuntarily participated in the cold weather research program, never survived the experiments or the research on weapons testing.

The "Plague program" was used on the general population. Researchers infected clothing and supplies with infected fleas that carried Cholera or anthrax or Bubonic plague and were put in plastic containers (bombs) and dropped on Chinese towns and cities such as Changde. The "International Symposium on Crimes of Bacteriological Warfare" estimated that 580,000 died in this manner. [46] [47]

In addition to the cruel and humane experiments, they conducted weapons testing on humans using flame throwers and grenades and biological and germ and chemical weapons. They even conducted research by injecting women and men with a virulent strain of syphilis to see how the organs in the body deteriorated, then perform a vivisection while the person was still alive. This was also performed on pregnant women as well. [48]

Ishii developed a plan called, "Operation Cherry Blossoms at Night". He planned to put fleas infected with bubonic plague in bombs and have Kamikaze bombers drop them on San Diego, California. It may seem far-fetched, but Ishii and his affiliate Unit 1644 had already dropped bombs on Ningbo in 1940 and Changde in 1941 with plague infested fleas which carried bubonic plague. Hundreds of thousands of civilians died as a result. Japan also used chemical and biological warfare on American troops in the islands in the Pacific. The deadline for bombing San Diego with bubonic plague was set for September, 22, 1945, however, Japan surrender on September 2, 1945 in which Ishii and his crew immediately flew back to Japan before the Soviets would find Unit 731 in Harbin, Manchuria. [53][47]

Ishii did not necessarily take pleasure in killing patients as Josef Mengele had, but he killed under the guise of science and research. In Ishii's mind, the end justified the means, even if it involved pain, suffering and torture of his patients; it was considered part of the research. Ishii was called, "The Doctor of Death" and for very good reason, no one could match his level of medical atrocities except maybe Vlad the Impaler in 1477.

It has been estimated that there may have been as many as 8 Units during World War II, but the exact number is not known because of the shroud of secrecy that exist today. Some of these units were for support or holding facilities for prisoners. Records indicate that as many as 250,000 people may have been subject to human experimentation during the war, under the guise of research. [57] This figure did not consider the deaths as a result of biological warfare experimentation on the general population in China.

After the surrender of Japan, Ishii's research team returned to Japan and resumed their research on human subjects and biological and chemical warfare. Most of the doctors under Ishii's unit later became prominent political leaders and owners of large pharmaceutical companies, Dean of Medical Schools, research professors, Ministers of Health and other high ranking positions within the Japanese government and educational institutions. [55]

Unit 731 occupied six square Kilometers and consisted of 150 buildings. At the end of the war in 1945, Ishii ordered the destruction of the compound and the death of 400 patients still incarcerated in Unit 731 holding cells. He gave orders to dispose of the storage containers of biological and chemical compounds into the city's water supply. Thousands of people died as a result in Harbin and other cities nearby. His purpose was to hide any evidence of the existence of chemical warfare from the Russians when they arrived. [60]

Human Research

The United States wasn't involved in human research until after World War II, and most of that research was to determine the effects of radiation on humans that had already been exposed to radiation, especially after the bombing of Hiroshima and Nagasaki in 1945. There were a few biological experiments carried out in Florida and the South, but nothing to the scale or carnage employed by Japan or Germany during World War II. Most of the experiments conducted in the United States rarely ended in the death to the patients, or at least not intentionally, however, in Japan, it was a different story.

After the bombing of Hiroshima and Nagasaki and the surrender of Japan on September 2, 1945, General Douglas MacArthur was appointed Supreme Commander of the Allied Forces in Japan. Rumors surfaced about Japan's human research and experimentation with biological and chemical warfare on cities in China. The United States wasn't sure about the extent of the biological and chemical warfare research program by Japan, and had only a broad suspicion based on rumors of the human experiments carried on in Ishii's Unit 731 and other Units during the war. They knew that the Japanese had used chemical warfare on some American troops fighting in the South Pacific, but was unaware of the extent of its use. When Japan surrendered in September of 1945, Ishii and his research staff fled to Japan, and left a core group behind to destroy the facility and the patients that remained incarcerated. Fortunately, the buildings were so well constructed and reinforced, they survived the demolition, however, the 400 patients were killed and their bodies burned in the incinerators that were at the facility. When the Soviets arrived at Unit 731, they immediately arrested all of the remaining doctors and military officials who remained at the facility.

In Japan, US Lieutenant Colonel Murray Sanders arrived in Yokohama in mid-September of 1945. Colonel Sanders was a microbiologist working for the US military on the biological weapons program. He wanted all the research data that Ishii and his associates had accumulated on biological, chemical research, but was not fully aware of the human experiments. The United States Government was naïve and perhaps ignorant about what had occurred in Unit 731 during the war, or may not have known that Unit 731 existed until after the war.

The Japanese vehemently denied they conducted human experiments. Meetings continued into mid and late September of 1945 in which they held firm that no human experiments had been conducted on people, but they acknowledged having research data on biological and chemical warfare experiments and would exchange the data for immunity from prosecution of war crimes. In 1949, the United States granted immunity from prosecution of 1,000 doctors and medical researchers for war crimes in exchange for their research data. Ishii turned over some of the research, but held off in providing research data on the vivisections and human medical experimentation data. During interviews, vague details emerged about human experiments from some of the doctors. This information and transcripts pertaining to crimes against humanity were buried in secret classified files in the Pentagon, which remains today. The Americans didn't need the biological and chemical research data as much as keeping the information out of the hands of the Soviets and out of review from Congress and the American people, so officials claim. [49] [55] [5]

In 1946, MacArthur and his staff received a memorandum from the Director of Chemical Warfare Service of the United States that read:

"...prosecuting would cramp the United States ability in the future to engaged in chemical warfare ourselves.." [60]

The Director didn't want to prosecute the Japanese for using chemical warfare, for fear that the United States may need to use chemical warfare sometime in the future. Americans continued to interrogating hundreds of doctors involved in Unit 731. The Soviets arrested doctors, medical personnel and top military officials and charged them as war criminals and crimes against humanity. The war crime trials took place in Khabarovsk, Soviet Union in 1949.

Twelve top military leaders and scientist from Unit 731 were convicted and served between two to 25 years in a Siberian labor camps. The United States did not acknowledge the trials, and called them communist propaganda. [55] [56]

General Douglas MacArthur, gave the Physicians of Unit 731 full immunity in exchange for their research data. [49]

The Corp Research and Development Command, Biological Warfare Laboratories in Maryland sent a memo that indicated they received the data. The memo read: "*....we got all of the information.   For $250,000, we got a bargain!*" [60]

It appears from the above memo that the United States was selling the information to other U.S. agencies. Ishii and his team continued with his research under the nose of General MacArthur's occupation in Japan but perhaps not on human experimentation. To this day, little is known about the atrocities which occurred in Unit 731, 100 and Unit 1644. Right wing Japanese politicians denied they it ever existed, and it appears that the United States did also.

On May 6, 1947, General Douglas MacArthur wrote Washington;

"additional data, possibly some statements from Ishii probably can be obtained by informing Japanese involved that information will be retained in intelligence channels and will not be employed as 'war crimes' evidence." [49]

The United States considers the information covert and classified, and the Japanese government claims: "No findings of fact about the existence of human experimentation".

The Battle of Manila

In March of 1945, the war in the Pacific was coming to an end and Douglas MacArthur wanted to be the first person to liberate Manila, as he vowed to do in 1941 when we was driven out of the Philippines by the Japanese. At that time, he reassured the Philippine people he would return and liberate them. General Yamashita gave orders to evacuate Manila; however, Admiral Sanji decided they should hold their ground in Manila with 10,000 Japanese marines and 4,000 regular troops. He thought that the Americans would not bombard Manila for fear of killing civilians and that his 14,000 troops could easily hold off the American troops. MacArthur approached Manila on 3 sides with a force of 35,000 troops. As American and Philippine troops began closing in on the business district of Manila, Admiral Sanji received an order from General Yamashita that read:

"The Americans who have penetrated into Manila have about 1,000 troops, and there are several thousand Filipino soldiers and organized guerrillas. Even women and children have become guerrillas. All people on the battlefield with the exception of Japanese military personnel, Japanese civilians, Special Construction Units will be put to death." [51]

The order continued,

"When Filipinos are to be killed, they must be gathered into one place and disposed of with the consideration that ammunition and manpower must not be used to excess. Because the disposal of dead bodies is a troublesome task, they should be gathered into houses which are scheduled to be burned or demolished. They should also be thrown into the river." [51]

Over the one month siege of the Battle of Manila, Japanese troops terrorized the civilian population with violent mutilations, rape and mass deaths in hospitals, schools, churches and colleges. In the end, more than 100,000 civilians died in the Massacre of Manila. During the War Crimes Tribunal, General Yamashita and Akira Muto were found guilty and were executed in 1946 and 1948 respectively for their crimes against humanity.

Operation Downfall

American entered the World War II on December 7, 1941 with the Japanese bombing Pearl Harbor, Hawaii. The war will end in the reverse order, by America bombing the Japanese cities of Hiroshima and Nagasaki on August 6th and 9th in 1945, just 5 years later.

The British began "Operation Dracula" in May for the liberation of Burma with help from the Burmese National Army. In the next few months more than 150,000 Japanese troops were killed and only about 2,000 surrendered. Australia was also having equal success in liberating Borneo and isolating Japanese troops in the Dutch East Indies which effectively took them out of the war. China with the help of America pushed the Japanese out of the north and out of their stronghold along the Yangtze River in China.

By the spring of 1945, American troops seized almost all of the islands in the western Pacific that were once held by the Japanese, including Iwo Jima and the bloodiest battle of them all; Okinawa and the Ryukyu Islands, which lay only 400 miles south of Kyushu, Japan. The battle of Okinawa lasted from April until the end of June of 1945. More than 117,000 Japanese were killed, and the Americans suffered 75,000 casualties plus another 5,000 US Navy casualties from the loss of 38 ships. Many of the navy casualties were the result of Kamikaze suicide bombing. The British Pacific Fleet was south of Okinawa protecting the American troops from a possible counter invasion from the south.

On May 8, 1945, the war in Europe ended with the surrender of Germany and Italy, however, the war in the Pacific was still going on in full force. Japan refused to sign an unconditional surrender after the Allied victory of Iwo Jima and Okinawa, which would put American bombers only 400 miles from Japans southern coast. Within weeks of taking Okinawa, plans were being made to move 3,000 B-29 bombers and 240 Squadrons of B-17 bombers into Okinawa and Iwo Jima. It would be part of "Operation Downfall".

The Joint Chief of Staff, Admiral Nimitz, General MacArthur, General Marshall and Truman and Secretary of War, Stimson, previously prepared casualty estimates of the amount of Allied casualties that could be expected. Truman wanted the first leg of the invasion to start no later than November 1, 1945. The estimated American and Allied casualties were staggering, in which most agreed that casualties could be as low as 450,000 and as high as 1.7 million allied troops killed during the invasion.

The use of the Atom bomb was never considered during the invasion plan strategy. Only President Truman and Stimson and a few top level officials had knowledge of the Manhattan Project. It was first tested in July of 1945 in New Mexico and the invasion plan had already been prepared by the time the nuclear tests were completed.

The plan involves two operations called Olympic and Coronet. Olympic was to invade the southern tip of Japan, which included the larger islands and the city of Kyushu. Okinawa would be used as a staging area or base of operation. Once the islands, ports and airports had been secured, it would provide the support for operation Coronet, in which troops would invade the Kanto Plain in the spring of 1946. Operation Coronet had a sub-operation called "Pastel". Its purpose was to plan a deception in which the Japanese would be convinced that America would not invade Tokyo and the Kanto Plain. The Coronet invasion would have been larger than the Normandy Invasion.

While American and British intelligence kept track of Japanese troop movements, they realized that the Japanese already knew the most likely locations for a likely allied invasion, and started moving troops from Manchuria, Korea and China into Kyushu on the southern tip of Japan. When Olympic was first proposed, intelligence reports indicated there were 180,000 Japanese troops on standby in Kyushu and another 420,000 north in Honshu. Near Tokyo, it was estimated that 280,000 troops were on standby in the Kanto Plain. However, intelligence reports indicated that in Kyushu, there were massive Japanese troop build-ups by the spring of 1945. American troops would be fighting not the previous prediction of 180,000, but at least 545,000 Japanese troops.

The Battle of Okinawa, April 1945   Fig. 3

It was also estimated that by November there could be as many as 900,000 troops. It would have a 1:1 fighting ratio between American and Japanese forces, which could mean defeat for the American forces, or at the very least, a massive casualty rate. It was a risk that Stimson and Truman didn't want to take.

Operation Meetinghouse

While Washington and the Joint Chief of Staff were trying to develop a less painless method to invade Japan, US Air Force General Curtis Lemay proposed another plan in January 1945. The bombing prior to 1945 was aimed primarily at destroying Japanese manufacturing but was having little effect. The Japanese moved many of their smaller manufacturing facilities to small workshops in rural villages and residential areas that didn't resemble manufacturing facilities and were less venerable to bombing. General Lemay wanted to use low level incendiary raids using hundreds of bombers to completely destroy entire cities. As LeMay had so eloquently put it;

"Why just swat at a few flies when we could go after the whole dung pile."

Even though America always preferred a soft policy, most felt that a hard-line policy at this point in the war was necessary to force Japan's surrender, especially since Japan's primary ally, Germany had already surrendered.

Lemay's reasoning was to destroy the Japanese ability to make weapons, airplanes, tanks and even food. To do so, he needed to shift from precision bombing to area bombing using incendiary bombs. In that way, should American be forced to invade the mainland, even if the Japanese had a large army, they had no way to support or defend themselves during the invasion of the mainland, or at least in theory.

On March 9, 1945, Operation Meetinghouse began with the bombing of Tokyo using incendiary bombs that lasted two days. The bombing destroyed 16 square miles of the city and 267,000 buildings in a single night. More than 100,000 people were killed. It was the single most deadly air raid of World War II. Over the next six months, 67 Japanese cities and 33 smaller towns were firebombed and completely destroyed using incendiary bombs. Most of the buildings were made of wood and rice paper, thus fire would spread until the entire city was in ashes. While the effects were devastating to the general population it had little effect on Japanese patriotism for the mother land.

The Manhattan Project

By 1943, the war had already been decided in the Pacific between America and Japan, even though the Japanese failed to see the handwriting on the wall, or at the very least acknowledged the loss, the United States was producing nearly 100,000 aircraft a month, whereas Japan had only produced 70,000 for the entire war. By 1944, the United States had 100 aircraft carriers and Japan only 25 for the entire war. The U.S. fleet had sunk so many Japanese cargo ships that the economy was in a spiraling decline, and manufacturing capabilities were nearing a standstill. But with all of the doom, the Japanese continued to fight, and couldn't imagine losing the war.

Japan realized that an American invasion was imminent, so they told the citizens to have available to them any item in the household that could be used as a weapon, such as knives, old swords or tools. It became clear that Japan did not have enough weapons to supply their citizen's for an effective militia.

Meanwhile, in 1939, a joint venture of scientist from, Canada, England and the United States were assembled in New Mexico for the purpose of creating the first nuclear bomb. It was called the Manhattan Project. The concept of nuclear fission was the brain child of two German chemists, Otto Hahn and Fritz Stresemann and Physicist, Lisa Meitner in 1938. [66]

Lisa Meitner was Jewish and the Professor of Physics at a prestigious German University working on nuclear fission. She fled Germany to live in Sweden when the University was ordered to report any Jewish academia working at the University. She continued her research by mail with Hahn and Stressemann. The United States wanted her to join the team on the Manhattan Project but she refused. For the next two years, there were scientific obstacles to be figured out, such as how much enriched Uranium to produce a bomb. The problem was solved by two British scientist in 1941 who presented their theory to the MAUD Committee (a scientific think tank in England), which eventually made its way to the scientist in New Mexico. They proposed to use about 2 pounds of uranium-235 and a neutron modulator called heavy water. This was a breakthrough for the scientist in the Manhattan Project, partly because they were expecting to use one ton of uranium for each bomb. [65]

By the spring of 1945, two different nuclear bombs were assembled, one was a nuclear fission bomb using uranium-235, called "Little Boy" , and the other was a nuclear fusion bomb using Plutonium, called "Fat Boy". The first test for the nuclear fission bomb took place at Alamogordo, New Mexico on July 16, 1945.

In April of 1945, even before the bomb was tested, a committee was formed to select potential targets for the detonation of the nuclear bomb. It was envisioned that once the first bomb (Little Boy) was dropped, the Japanese would surrender, however, if they didn't, they would use the second and more powerful bomb "Fat Boy", which was 20% more powerful than "Little Boy".

The Target Committee selected five cities which had not been previously fire bombed. The first target was Kokura, which had Japan's largest munitions plant and the second target was Hiroshima, which had a large military headquarters located in the city and was also a large embarkation port. The next target was Yokohama, which had a large aircraft manufacturing facility, oil refineries, machine tools and electrical equipment plant. Niigata had oil refineries, industrial manufacturing of steel and aluminum, and lastly Kyoto, which was a major industrial center.

Surprisingly, Nagasaki was not on the original target committees list. Kyoto was spared from the list because Henry Stimson, Secretary of Defense, had his honeymoon in Kyoto and thought it was too beautiful to bomb, so Nagasaki replace Kyoto on the list. [65]

There was considerable debate as to whether the United States should give Hirohito adequate notice and intent that the United States intended to drop a doomsday bomb on Japan if they didn't surrender. Some suggested dropping fliers to give adequate notice, but others felt that if notice were given, they would be forewarned and intercepted by bombers before they reached their target, thus ruining the element of surprise. Also, it was believed that the Japanese would move prisoners of war to the suspected target cities. Both were valid arguments, so it was decided not to forewarn of the pending bombing. However, the United States did drop 63 million fliers suggesting that there will be continued bombings that would devastate their cities unless Japan surrenders. Japan announced that anyone caught with a flyer would be punished by death. So even if they dropped the notices, it was illegal for Japanese citizens to read or have fliers in their possession.

On July 26, 1945, the United States submitted the terms of conditional surrender to Japan, which was rejected repeatedly. Japan wanted four conditions of their surrender:

1   That the Imperial government remain intact

2   Japan not be occupied

3   Japan's armed forces be disbanded voluntarily

4   War criminals be prosecuted in Japanese courts

All four of these conditions were not acceptable to the Allies. [65]

Realizing that Japan had no intension of surrendering, Truman and Sir Winston Churchill decided that the only option was to drop a nuclear bomb on Japan. It had already been scheduled for August 6, 1945. The first city would be Hiroshima with Nagasaki and Kokura as secondary targets.

The 393rd Bombardment Squadron of B-29's were stationed in Tinian Island, near Saipan. It was a 6 hour flight to Japan. The B-29, named "Enola Gay" was the name given to the plane by Colonel Paul Tibbets. It was named after his grandmother, Enola Gay. On August 6, 1945, the Enola Gay would rendezvous with three other support bombers in Iwo Jima. Hiroshima had a population of 381,000 people and on the morning of August 6th, the weather was clear. [65]

Japanese radar picked up five separate bombing squadrons heading south but at midnight of August 6th the alert was over. At 8:15 am of the morning of August 6, the bombardier, Major Thomas Ferebee dropped "Little Boy" on Hiroshima. [65]

The results were devastating. 70,000 to 80,000 people were killed, of which, 20,000 were military. It was estimated that 30% of the population of the city were killed. Even with the devastation, Japan refused to surrender. [65]

On August 9, 1945, the B-29 named "Boxcar" piloted by Major Charles Sweeney left Tinian Island at 3:49 am with the nuclear fission bomb called "Fat Boy" in route to Kokura. Once again "Boxcar" would rendezvous with three support B-29's, of which one would be the "Enola Gay", which would provide weather reconnaissance. [65]

During the flight to Kokura, a crewman notified the Pilot that there was a problem with a fuel transfer pump and they were unable to transfer 640 gallons into the aircraft fuel tanks. Sweeney decided to continue the flight and after the bombing would land in Okinawa rather than go back to Tinian Island as planned. When arriving at Kokura, it was shrouded in smoke from aerial bombardment the night before. They made three attempts to locate their target and decided to go to the secondary target in Nagasaki. At 7:50 am over Nagasaki, air raid alerts were sounded, but an all clear alarm was sounded at 8:30am. At 11:01 am bombardier, Captain Kermit Beahan dropped the first plutonium nuclear bomb on Nagasaki. It exploded 1,650 feet above the ground. "Boxcar" was dangerously low on fuel and made a dash to Okinawa. When he arrived at Okinawa, one engine sputtered out of fuel and another quit while landing, but made a safe landing. [65]

It was unknown exactly how many were killed as a result of the bomb, but it was estimated that 40,000 to 80,000 died. At least eight prisoners of war were killed in the blast. [65]

Two more "Fat Man" plutonium fusion bombs were now ready in New Mexico. They were scheduled to be dropped on August 11th and 14th. [65]

In Tokyo, after hearing about Nagasaki being bombed, a story was told that a prisoner of war being held in a Tokyo prison was interrogated after the bombing. He was repeatedly asked how many nuclear bombs did America have. Of course the pilot knew nothing, but to avoid being beaten or tortured, he told his captures that America had about 100 from what he had heard. The interrogators immediately told their superiors and the following day the Japanese sent a letter of surrender.

I haven't been able to confirm this story as true or not, but if it were true, this prisoner may have saved thousands of lives. In fact, America had only two nuclear plutonium fusion bombs left after Nagasaki, because Colonel Paul Tibbets was given the order to fly to New Mexico and bring two nuclear bombs back to Tinian

Island. His orders were cancelled a few days later after the informal surrender of Japan.

Even today, the debate continues over the use of the nuclear bomb. President Eisenhower thought the use of the atomic bomb wasn't necessary, since Japan was defeated anyway. I suppose he is correct, however, in the eyes of the Japanese, they were not defeated, and far from it. When Hirohito announced the surrender, riots broke out in Japan by those who would not accept surrender at any price or at any cost to human life.

From the American's point of view, they were concerned that if the war continued, the Soviet Union had already expressed an interest in advancing into the Kurile Islands and perhaps the northern mainland of Japan itself. The Kurile Island lay only miles off the coast of Northern Japan. It was obvious, that the Soviets entered the war just days before the surrender of Japan for the primary purpose of taking the Islands and with hopes of getting some of the spoils of war in Asia. They already advanced into North Korea so it was important for the United States to take full control of Japan since Russia contributed nothing in the War in the Pacific. In the long run, the nuclear bomb, as bad as it may have been, may have been Japan's ultimate savor. If the Soviet Army invaded Japan, Russia would have more than likely wanted to divide Japan in half like Korean or Vietnam.

This would eventually, in time set the stage for Japan wanting reunification and most certainly another war. Russia claimed the Kurile Island after the war, but America wasted little time in establishing a new government in Japan. In 1951, the United States turned Japan over to self-rule to Emperor Hirohito.

As a result of the war, Japan lost some of it territories, Taiwan and South Korea and North Korea. They would later become independent States, after being rule by Japan for more than 35 years. Taiwan would later be annexed by China.

Nagasaki, August 9, 1945   Fig. 4

The cost in human life was another prime consideration for dropping the atomic bombs on Japan. Casualty estimates prepared by the War Department, Joint Chief of Staff and others, summarized that as many as 1 million or more American may lose their lives had we invaded Japan. Some estimates were higher. But some estimated that 15 million Japanese would be killed in the invasion, mostly civilians. The reason the estimates were high was due to the ferocity of the fighting in Okinawa and Iwo Jima, and their unwillingness to surrender, even when it was hopeless to continue.

Before the battle of Okinawa, the Japanese began moving troops into the southern tip of Japan, expecting an American and British invasion force landing in Kyushu. Japan was not prepared to ever surrender, however the atomic bomb was the deciding factor for Japans premature surrender. Had the atomic bombs not been dropped, America could expect the war to continue for another two years at the very least. The question still remains as to whether the use of the atomic bomb started a nuclear proliferation or was it a necessary evil that may have thwarted the future use of it.

Chapter 5

China: Rise of the Red Dragon

Sun Yet-Sen was born in 1866, in the village of Cuiheng, China. When he was 13, he went to live with his brother, Sun Mei, in Honolulu, Hawaii. He acquired a Hawaiian birth certificate, which allowed him to travel freely in and out of the United States. After graduation, he moved back to his home in Cuiheng, China, but shortly after arriving he had gotten in trouble with the local police and fled to Hong Kong. While there, he enrolled into college and eventually acquired a medical degree. While attending college, he began to attend meetings held by the "Revive China Society", which advocated the overthrow of the Qing Dynasty with hopes of installing a Democracy in China.

After graduation from medical school, he became active in political groups advocating nationalizing China. In 1894, he returned to Hawaii to gather support for his nationalist movement and over the next 12 years, Sun Yat-Sen took part in at least 8 failed attempts to over throw the Qing Dynasty. During one failed attempt, as many as 70 of his fellow Nationalist were rounded up by the government, however, Sun Yat-Sen managed to flee to Japan before being caught.

A turning point in the events occurred in 1908, when Emperor Guangxu died of poisoning, and on the very next day, Empress Dowager Cixi also died of an apparent poisoning. In 1908, Puyi (Xuantong) was 2 years old and became the next heir as Emperor of China. The Empress

Dowager Longyu adopted Puyi and managed his affairs of State until he became an adult.

In October of 1911, Sun Yat-Sen was in exile and lived in Japan and the United States when the Xinhai Revolt broke-out in Wuchang. He rushed back to China when he heard the news that the Qing Dynasty had fallen. He became the Provisional President of the newly formed Republic of China; however there was one major obstacle in his way, the Emperor Puyi.

General Yuan Shi-Kai requested Puyi to abdicate his throne, in which Yuan offered the Dowager Empress 1,700 pounds of silver if she would stamp the Royal Edict of the Abdication of the Emperor Puyi, which she eagerly accepted.

Yuan Shi-Kai was a northern war lord who later became a General in the Qing Dynasty Empire. The Nationalist promised Yuan the Presidency of the newly formed Republic of China if he would help over-throw the Qing Dynasty. The liberation front made concessions to Yuan Shi-Kai in exchange of bring down the Dynasty. Without Yuan's to support it was not possible to overthrow the Dynasty.

After the fall of the Qing Dynasty, Sun Yat-Sen turns over the Presidency to Yuan Shi-Kai. The Nationalist's formed the first legislative assembly in which half of the seats were pro Sun Yat-Sen and the other half were pro Yuan Shi-Kai. During the assembly meeting, Sun Yat-Sen officially named the Kuomintang (KMT) party and Song Jiao-Ren was elected party President. Yuan soon realized that the KMT party was becoming too powerful and influential for him to control and realized it possible may be voted out as President at the whim of the Party. Yuan Shi-Kai orders the assassination of KMT President, Song Jiao-Ren. A party conflict ensues between the two-party factions. The war lord, Yuan and his superior army forces Sun Yat-sen to flee to Japan in exile.

This was the start of the Bai Lang Rebellion in which the war lords fought to take control of the newly formed Republic of China. While the drama was unfolding with Yuan Shi-Kai, Sun Yat-Sen wanted to overthrow the self-proclaimed Emperor, Yuan Shi-Kai, who had assassinated his closest friend and leader of the Kuomintang party, Song Jiao-Ren.

Yuan's army was much too large to over-throw, so he turned to the Communist Party of China and Soviet leader, Lenin for support. Two years later, in 1916, General Yuan Shi-Kai declares himself Hong Xian Emperor of China, but dies only 3 months later of liver failure. But, because Sun Yat-Sen had contacted the Communist party for help, they had formed an alliance which lasted until his death in 1925.

In 1924, Sun Yat-Sen appointed a young military Officer as Commandant of the National Revolutionary Army. His name was Chiang Kai-Shek. With Soviet Aid, they were able to train and recruit 200,000 for an attack against the three war lords in the Northeast, Central Plains and the Manchurian regions, but during the attacks, Sun Yet-Sen dies of liver cancer and Chiang Kai-Shek takes command and becomes leader of the Kuomintang (KMT).

Chiang Kai-Shek disliked communist, so his first order of business was to purge the KMT of all Communist and communist sympathizers. This was a decision which would later haunt him, because it was the Communist who trained and supplied most of the troops and provided the money to fight the war lords for control over much of North and Central China.

Mao Zedong worked for the Kuomintang as a political organizer in Shanghai in 1925, along with Zhou

Enlai, Zhu De and Lin Biao. After the purge, the four joined the small yet well-organized Chinese Communist Party (CCP) in Shanghai. Chiang Kai-Shek's support had gradually dwindled and his hatred for the communist became an obsession.

The Long March

In 1934, Chiang Kai-Shek's army had grown to over 700,000 soldiers. The United States provided Chiang Kai-shek's KMT Party Military aid and armament and aircraft. Mao, on the other hand, had only a force of about 300,000, which were scattered in small battalions and regiments in remote areas throughout southwestern China. His ploy was to you guerrilla warfare of hit and run. Chiang Kai-Shek pushed Mao's main force of 86,000 out of the Shanghai region and into a remote area in southwest China. The Nationalist encircled the communist positions and built concrete fortification around the Communist strong-hold to form a blockade, thus depriving them of supplies and food. Thousands died as a result of starvation and exhaustion. In October of 1934, the communist realized they had to break out of the encirclement else slowly be annihilated. They found a weak spot in the encirclement and slipped out under the cover of darkness without Chiang Kai-sheiks knowledge. Mao's main force of 86,000 soldiers and 15,000 non-military support personnel and 35 women headed west. While crossing the Hsiang River in November of 1934, they encountered Nationalist fortifications. After heavy fighting, they lost nearly 50,000 soldiers, but were able to break through and continue the march northwest.

When Mao's Red Army reached the Dadu River, Chiang Kai-sheik's Nationalist Army was waiting on the opposite side of the river. Neither army was able to cross the raging rapids of the Dadu River. The Commander of the Red Army, Yang Chengwu and his second in command, Mao's trusted friend, Lin Biao knew they had to cross the Lui Ting Bridge, 80 miles upstream before Chiang Kai-sheks army and warlords arrived before him, so he gave the order to take Liu Ting Bridge as quickly as possible before Chiang Kai-sheks main force arrives.

Lin Biao marched his troops day and night up-river until they arrived at the bridge. The bridge was an ancient bridge constructed of sixteen iron chains that were anchored and cemented into the rocks on each side of the river. It had a span of about 300 feet with heavy wooden planks spanning between the steel chains for a deck. When Lin Biao arrived with his army they found that the War lords had removed half of the deck planking. On the opposite side was a machine gun nest positioned and concealed in the rock cliff. Lin Biao asked for volunteers to cross the bridge to "take-out" the machine gun nest. Thirty volunteers stepped forward, with each having a rifle and hand grenades strapped to their backs. There were snipers positioned on the cliffs shooting at the red volunteers as they attempted to cross.

After half of the men were shot, they finally reached the decking and were able to crawl and their way within range to the machine gun emplacement and able to toss a grenades that destroyed the machine gun nest. A commander for the Nationalist gave the command to remove the remainder of the planking, but it was too late, half of the volunteers were able to hold down the small detachment of Nationalist. As the Red soldiers started to cross the bridge to assist the Red volunteers, the Nationalist tossed paraffin fire balls on the planking with the hope of burning the planking before the main force was able to cross, but this effort failed and soon the Red Army took the bridge.

Over the next year, Mao encountered daily skirmishes and battles in which he incurred heavy losses.

His troops reached the tallest mountain range and was forced to ascend over the top of the 15,000 foot mountains and down into the grass plains and marsh lands of China's great plains near the border of Russia. When they finally reached Shensi, they were met by a small garrison of red army troops and the long march was over. Mao's army had crossed 24 rivers, 18 mountain ranges and had only about 6,000 soldiers left. He marched his troops more than 6,000 miles.

Some historians claim that the battle of Lui Ting Bridge may not have taken place at all. Some believe it may have been a propaganda ploy to bolster Mao's "bigger than life" image, since there were no witnesses to authenticate the event, other than Lin Biao and Mao. There are a few who fought in the Battle of Lui Ting City, but weren't present during the battle for Lui Ting Bridge. Chairman Deng Xiaoping claimed it was an "over exaggeration". Historical facts supports that the long march did exist and confirms that of the 86,000 soldiers who started on the trek, only 6,000 arrived in Shensi. What isn't known is how many were killed and how many deserted the effort.

When World War II broke-out and the Japanese invaded China, both KMT and CCP joined forces and fought a guerrilla war against the Japanese. The CCP was the primary military force against the Japanese, while the KMP elected to avoided skirmishes with the Japanese. Chiang Kai-Shek's strategy was to let the Japanese destroy the CCP which would be an easy victory for him. This military strategy would however back fire after the Japanese pulled-out of China.

The KMT on the other hand, lost support and trust of the Chinese people, partly because Chiang Kai-Shek made a "backdoor" deal with the Japanese to remain in China after the war to help fight the communist, and as it happened, many did volunteer to fight as mercenaries for the Nationalist under Chiang Kai-shek.

Enlisting the Japanese built a resentment toward the KMT among the Chinese population. Almost all of the Chinese wanted the Japanese out of China at any cost, regardless of their intention or motives. The Chinese viewed Chiang Kai-Shek's concession as a betrayal and created a deep distrust that it may have led to the ultimate down fall of the KMT.

The support for the CCP grew steadily during the war, while Chiang Kai-shek's support dwindled, as a result of his collusion with the Japanese. There were rumors of wide-spread corruption within KMT's leadership which certainly did not help his credibility.

Mao's Army in the Long March of 1934, *Fig. 6*

The CCP went from village to village and offered protection and support to the villagers with the harvest of rice. The CCP used this opportunity to remind the people that Chiang Kai-shek was pro-Japanese, which was not necessarily the case. By 1945, Chiang Kai-Shek relied entirely on aid from the United States with the help Mao's wife, Soong May-ling, who was the sister-in-law of Sun Yat-Sen and would become an American citizen. She campaigned relentlessly for financial support from the U.S. Congress and American businesses to fight the Chinese Communist. Jokingly, the Americans called him "General Cash my Check". But, because of money and foreign aid pouring in, so did corruption which grew proportionately with the amount of money they received from sponsors in the United States. Corruption was widespread among most KMT officials, in which support would eventually begin to "dry-up". Without a sizeable army, they were pushed out of mainland China and by 1948; Mao Zedong and the People's Republic of China seized power and control of Mainland China. Chiang Kai-Shek and his nationalist army would flee to the Island of Formosa.

China, under the leadership of Mao Zedong, had defeated the Nationalist and became the largest communist nation in Asia and the most populated. Because of China's size and population, Stalin was distrustful and paranoid of Mao, and always remained at arm's length in his relationship with him. Mao once traveled to Moscow for a meeting with Stalin to sign an Alliance agreement between the two countries, but Stalin made Mao wait two days before seeing him. Mao was furious which set the tone of distrust between China and Russia that would last until Mao's death in 1976, long after the death of Stalin.

Taiwan (Formosa)

The United States continued their support of Chiang Kai-Shek and provided economic and military aid to Taiwan. Chiang Kai-shek was viewed as a freedom fighter by the United States and served as a tool to fight communism. America wasn't concerned about human rights as long as it coincides with America's policy and agenda to rid Asia of communism.

There was a growing concern in the United States that Chiang Kai-Shek was more of a dictator than a freedom fighter or a combination of both. Soon after Chiang Kai-Shek fled to Taiwan, he failed to carry out the principals he and Sun Yat-Sen's espoused.

As with many self-proclaimed freedom fighters, most of the money went into the pockets of government officials and little went toward fighting communism or to elevate poverty in Taiwan. He failed to embrace free elections as promised and became obsessed with cleansing Communist from Taiwan, even though there were very few. He continued with his attacks in Taiwan with hopes of maintaining his image as a freedom fighter against communism, which would guarantee foreign aid from the United States.

Even though the Republic of China (Taiwan) wrote a constitution, the government remained a one party system, run by Chiang Kai-Shek and his select group from mainland China. The country was under martial law and he failed to enact the certain civil rights such as free speech, the right of assembly and other Constitutional guarantees during his reign, which lasted until 1987.

To insure that the communist didn't take over Taiwan, Chiang Kai-Shek implemented the "White Terror" in which more than 140,000 Taiwanese were rounded-up and imprisoned for their real or perceived opposition of the Kuomintang and nationalism. He used the "White Terror" technique in China during his reign in China before fleeing to Taiwan. Like the Cultural Revolution in China, the White Terror was also used as a political tool to rid political opponents whom they felt may become a political threat or undermine his authority.

The White Terror

Little was known in the West about what went on during the period of the White Terror in Taiwan, which lasted from 1949 to 1987. With government censorship, it was forbidden to talk or write or even discuss events inside Taiwan.

Ban Rak Thai, Thailand. Chinese Kuomintang refugees fled communist China in 1949 and established their own towns in border regions of Indochina. Fig 7

To help purge the communist and political adversaries, the government offered incentives to the arresting officer, which allowed them to seize their personal assets including their wife in some cases, if they were suspected of being a subversive or anti-nationalist. Thousands were incarcerated and sent to forced labor camps such as Green Island, off the coast of Taiwan. Those arrested endured torture and forced to sign false confessions that named friends, family and enemies who may be sympathetic to communism. During the interrogation, most named anyone just to keep from being tortured. similar in context to and Pol Pot in S-21 prison in Cambodia and the Red Fear in America.

The actual number of communist and subversives captured were relatively low, perhaps a few hundred, but the generous incentives offered by the government made affluent Taiwanese easy targets. It is not known how many died or how many were executed during the reign of the White Terror, but some estimates are 3,000 to 4,000 were victims. Even after the death of Chiang Kai-Shek, his Vice President, Yen Chia-Kan, continued the White Terror until his death in 1987.

The United States didn't get involved in the White Terror in Taiwan, even though America was providing substantial aid, military weapons and aircraft to Taiwan. They turned a "Blind eye" to Taiwan. In 1953 the United States was having their own Red Terror against the communist and was in no position to criticize others about their methods of purging communist. In the U.S. Congress, Joe McCarthy was waging his own private war against what he perceived as the growing communist threat and infiltration of Communist into American society. Now the victims of the White Terror can speak openly without fear of reprisal, we are now beginning to learning about the terror that was inflicted upon the people under the guise of democracy.

Chiang Kai-Shek believed that corruption was the primary cause for his loss to the communist, but in reality, he and his cadre's made poor military decisions that gave the communist a big advantage. Like so many dictators and military generals who take control of countries, they may be good military leaders, but poor administrators and financial managers.

Many fled to the United States during Chiang Kai-Shek purge, but in fact it wasn't corruption he was addressing, but rather the elimination of his political rivals.

Corruption had always been a part of Chiang Kai-Shek's Kuomintang Party from the very start in China. Chiang Kai-Shek would die in 1975, at the age of 87, after ruling Taiwan for 26 years. He never realized his dream of reuniting Mainland China. Mao, his nemesis, would die one year later.

Now that Mao prevailed in war and had all of China to his own, he would soon learn that running a revolution and spear-heading a cause would not be enough to run a country successfully. By the second year, China wasn't able to produce enough food to feed 300 million people he forced into communes and the 500 million that lived in the cities. Wide spread famine followed during the winters of 1960 to 1963, in which millions would die of starvation and some even resorted to cannibalism to survive.

Mao had no choice but to return to an economic free market system, but he would never accept the fact that his Communist vision was a failure. In 1963, Chairman Mao stepped down as Chairman of the People's Republic of China and appointed Lui Shao qi as Chairman. After Lui Shao qi took over, he moved slowly toward a market economy where he did not rely on the collective communes to provide 100% of the food. Within one year, the economy and food supply doubled from the previous year, which proved that a market economic system would work and Mao's Great Leap Forward was a dismal failure.

The Cultural Revolution

The Cultural Revolution was an event in history orchestrated by Mao Zedong who wanted the people to rise-up against government, the educated, landlords and capitalist "roaders" whom he felt was the cause of his failure of his "Great Leap Forward". He was also gradually being sidelined as the leader of China which distressed him.

Millions of young people participated in a massive purge of death and mayhem under the orders of Mao Zedong, who had the cult following and cult personality to whip millions of people into a revolutionary frenzy overnight. By 1959, he had stepped down, but was still politically active in running the Party from the sidelines, but the Politburo was gradually giving Mao a secondary role in the political decisions. His programs for communism and a collective agrarian society had failed and Mao's relationship with Chairman Lui Shao qi had eroded. Lui Shao qi wanted China to modernize and abandon collective farming all together and adopt an economic based supply and demand system. Lui Shao qi once told Mao, "People are writing books about cannibalism in China". His belief was shared by Deng Xiaoping. Mao realized he needed to do something to turn misfortunes into good fortune and take back the power he once had. His most trusted and loyal confidants were not true believers in Marxism he felt and something had to change to restore his credibility with the people. It didn't bother Mao that millions perished from famine as a result of his domestic policies. He felt strongly that they failed as a result of not producing enough food to stave off starvation. He believed a cultural revolution was needed to purge the non-believers and "Capitalist Roaders" out of government and society, while monopolize his power and destroy his enemies. In the summer of 1966, he published an article in the Communist Party newspaper demanding that the people revolt and begin a new revolution of change. He published his red book of poems and verses and gave them to all those who follow him into revolution.

Mao made speeches at the Central Committee declaring the Great Proletarian Cultural Revolution shall begin. He ordered young people to become Red Guards, to purge anyone who was counter revolutionary, including the "Capitalist Roader" in government. Schools were closed and young red book revolutionaries called Red

Guards, were given free train rides to travel throughout China to hunt down the affluent and educated and counter revolutionaries and capitalist roaders. No one was safe from the Red Guard, not even the Chairman of the Communist Party, Lui Shao qi. He and Deng Xiaoping were arrested and taken in custody where Lui Shao qi and his wife were beaten and tortured and put into prison. Lui Shao qi was diabetic and was refused medication and would die in prison. His wife was humiliated in public and would spend 12 years in prison.

Deng Xiaoping was sent into exile in a labor camp in his rural village, but was spared his life, but his son was less fortunate and was tortured and thrown off a 5 story building and paralyzed.

The Red Guard removed the local and Provincial Party Committee officials and replaced them with Red Guard radicals. Mao replaced the Communist Central Committee with radical Red Guards as well. His most trusted and loyal communist friends were tortured and imprisoned and reports were received at Party headquarters of stories of cannibalism in the town of Wuxuan in Guangxi Province. The affluent and educated were killed and their livers and hearts were being eaten and shared with the villagers. One government report states that 137 people were killed and cannibalize by the residents of a small village in the Guangxi Provence.

As the intensity of the Cultural Revolution continued to rein terror on the government and its citizens, Mao couldn't stop the carnage and chaos. Few outside the bamboo curtain knew little of what was happening in China, since all communications to the outside world was cut-off. Finally in 1968, martial law was declared by Lin Biao who sent armed troops into Tiananmen Square to break-up the masses who had gathered each day. The military began beating and shooting protesters who Mao first ordered to rebel against the establishment in the first place.

Mao was obsessed with Marxism and believed it was the only system that would work. Frequent border clashes began along the Chinese and Russian borders and tensions started to developed between Russia's leader, Nikita Khrushchev and Mao. As a retaliatory gesture, Mao hinted toward normalizing relationships with the USA. Some speculated that the dispute with the Soviets in 1960 was the result of the Soviets refusing to give Mao military arms and weapons because of the instability in China during the cultural revolution. At one point during the cultural revolution, Nikita Khrushchev contacted Washington and wanted to know what the U.S. would do if Soviet Union attacked China and destroyed China's nuclear arsenal. Soviets had grave concerns about China. The Soviets were concerned that China's nuclear arsenal could fall in the hands of the radical red guard who seems to be running the government, while Mao just looked on.

As previously mentioned, martial law was ordered by Lin Biao, but it was viewed by Mao as a "power grab", since he wanted the revolution to run its course. Mao took measures to cut off Lin Biao as a possible successor. There were conspiracy theories that Lin Biao was planning to over-throw Mao and several months later news reports surfaced claiming that Lin Biao and his family were killed in a plane crash in Mongolia while attempting to flee to Russia. The real truth about Mao's closest confidant may never be known, recent reports confirmed that Lin Biao's plane was actually returning from Moscow when the plane crashed in Mongolia. The People of China loved Mao, but for those who were closest to him, never really know him or trusted him.

The Gang of Four

During the end of the Cultural Revolution in 1972, Mao suffered a serious stroke and seldom appeared in public. Almost all of his closest friends and confidants had been purged, murdered or imprisoned during the Cultural Revolution, except Zhou Enlai and Deng Xiaoping, who were the last of remaining survivors of the original Communist Party. Mao's wife, Jiang Qing and Wang Hongwen, Yao Wenyuan and Zhang Chunquio were party officials from Shanghai who moved-up into the communist party hierarchy during the Cultural Revolution, and became very powerful in their respective positions in government.

Mao's biggest leadership weakness was his lack of trust and his paranoia, but allowed his wife to assume much of the control of the party, which had gone unchecked during the Cultural Revolution. As a result, the Gang of Four gained control of government during the chaos. No one dared to speak harshly Jiang Qing. Jiang Qing was known to have a dominate personality and violent temper, so many feared her. Mao decided to bring back his longtime confidant, Deng Xiaoping from exile, because the country was in state of financial disarray as a result of years of turmoil and no manufacturing and industry being completely shut-down. He knew Deng was the only one who could get China back on its feet, even though he was "capitalist roader".

Zhou Enlai became ill and died of cancer in the spring of 1976, but the radicals, led by the Gang of Four, convinced Mao to once again exile Deng Xiaoping because of his pro nationalist beliefs. Deng told the Gang of Four after learning of the plan to deposed him again said;

"I have been deposed before; do you think I am afraid of being deposed again?"

Six months after the death of Zhou Enlai, Chairman Mao appoints Hua Guofeng as his successor, who was a

Department administrator at the time. After a lengthy illness, Mao Zedong dies on September 9, 1976 and Hu Guofeng took over as Party Chairman. His first order of business was to arrest the Gang of Four and reinstate Deng Xiaoping a Party Chairman.

The public trial of the Gang of Four was held in 1981 and was seen by millions on television. They were charged with treason and crimes against the State and charged with the deaths of 34,000 during the Cultural Revolution and 750,000 deaths as a result of starvation. They were all convicted and sentenced to 12 to 30 years in prison. The leader, Mao's wife, Jiang Qing received a life sentence, but would hang herself two years later while serving her prison sentence.

After Mao's death, Hua Guofeng became Party Chairman and gave up his position 1978 to Zhao Zayang, who only served three years. Deng Xiaoping became Party Chairman in 1981 and remained Party Chairman for the next 20 years.

Mao believed that the death of millions was the result of the people not having a firm conviction in the cause of Communism. He believed each were responsible for their own destiny and was instrumental in the death of 38 to 67 million people as a result of starvation, torture, imprisonment during his reign from 1949 to 1976. In the end, he died alone and friendless. The true legacy of Mao Zedong is only in the hearts of the people, but in reality he was a tyrant who lacked compassion for the people he ruled over.

Under the new capitalist economic system the people prospered beyond anyone's imagination. But, for China and the United States, there will always be problems to overcome. Perhaps the biggest obstacle will be trust, which will be the most difficult of all. China has become a major industrial nation in the past 25 years. But, like

Japan in the 1930's, industrial development requires natural resources to maintain its current level of growth and industrialization. What China seriously lacks is natural resources and what they can't purchase they may be forced to expand their borders like Japan did Germany did in the 1930's. As the Chinese proverb says;

"Without rice, even the cleverest housewife cannot cook"

Chapter 6

Korea: The First Juche

Imperial Japan ruled Korea and Taiwan (Formosa) from 1910 to 1945, but after the defeat of Japan in World War II, Formosa and Korea was given independence after 35 years under Imperial Japanese rule. During the war, 35% of the Japanese labor force, (2.6 million Koreans), were conscripted into Japanese society and by 1941, nearly 300,000 fought for Japan against the Allies. During the Cairo Conference in 1943, China, United Kingdom and the United States agreed that at wars end, Korea and Formosa would become independent States.

Stalin promised after the defeat of Germany, he would join Allied forces in the Pacific to fight the Japanese. Such a kind gesture from Stalin for ulterior motives for acquiring more real estate. Russia declared war against Japan on August 9, 1945, but on the following day, August 10th, Red troops marched into the Korean Peninsula. Stalin knew that the war in Japan was soon over; as a result of the United States dropping a nuclear bomb on Hiroshima three days before and on Nagasaki on the same day Russia declared war on Japan. It was certainly not a coincidence, since the United States gave advanced warning to all its allies, which include Russia.

On August 10th, American Colonels Dean Rusk and Charles Bonesteel, divided Korea into two zones, one managed by American and the other by the Soviet Union at the 38th parallel. It was made part of Japan's terms of surrender on August 15, 1945. Stalin kept his word, and stopped his Red Army from advancing beyond the 38th parallel until U.S. Forces arrived. Japan accepted the surrender of South Korea below the 38th parallel on September 8, 1945, and the United States Army Military Government of Korea took control of South Korea under a trusteeship.

The physical occupation of U.S. Forces would last three years, but the trusteeship with America would take five years. This arrangement was not popular with Koreans who had experienced 35 years under foreign domination. Riots and uprisings continued for several years, even during July of 1948 when Syngman Rhee was elected President of The Republic of South Korea. The Soviets installed a communist government in North Korea which was to be led by Kim Il-sung. In 1948, the Soviet Union withdrew its troops from North Korea as promised and the U.S. troops withdraw in 1949.

The Korean War

The ink hadn't dried on South Korea's Constitution when in the spring of 1950; North Korea invaded South Korea past the 38th parallel and into Seoul. **[Footnote 6]**

The new government of South Korea moved the center of Government further south, out of harm's way. There were only token U.S. Military troops in Korea at the time of the invasion, so it was a "cake walk" for the red army, since the South Korean troops had dwindled its forces from 100,000 in mid-summer to only 25,000 at the time of the invasion. A small American force was sent from Japan to Pusan in the south, which was the largest deep water port in Korea. Holding Pusan was an essential port for military supplies and military troop's deployment into South Korea.

To understand the Korean War, it's important to understand who the key players were. The North Korean President, Kim Il-sung was a puppet ruler installed by Stalin. Stalin installed Kim Il-sung as President because of his active role in fighting the Japanese during their occupation of the Korean Peninsula. Kim fled to Russia in World War II and returned as President of North Korea at the end of the war.

As the small US garrison was holding onto a fifty mile parameter around Pusan, the North Korean's were unable to take advantage of the opportunity and concentrated its army around Seoul, which would later prove to be a military blunder. The North Korean's needed to secure Pusan Harbor so that an invasion force could not land and get a foot hold on the Peninsula. Stalin was livid when he learned that Kim Il- sung ignored his Soviet military advisors who made it clear to take Pusan at all cost and not to worry about Seoul because it had little military importance.

The North Korean Army advanced with lightening speed across the DMZ and into South Korea and over powered South Korean defenses, but at a cost of over running their own resupply line. Soon the North Korean troops were out of food and ammunition and had no air support to counter the constant bombardment of the few UN forces that remained in South Korea. In 1950, Zhou Enlai had only four battalions along the border of North Korea and China. Kim Il-sung's initial drive into South Korea was a success, but would be short lived.

Zhou Enlai told Kim Il-sung;

"not to start celebrating too soon, the American forces hadn't arrived yet."

When UN and American forces arrived several months later under the commanded of General Douglas

MacArthur, who landed the bulk of his force on the coast of Incheon, and Pusan, so he could cut-off and trap the enemy troops behind the 38th parallel. MacArthur pushed his troops north past the 38th parallel deep into North Korea. This tactic worked, and Kim Il-sung pleaded with the Chinese and the Soviets to bring more troops in case the American UN forces decided to advance deeper into North Korea and take the capital.

Stalin and Zhou Enlai were out-raged over Kim Il-Sun's poor military leadership and judgment. China agreed to commit nearly 250,000 combat troops to North Korea, but stipulated that Kim Il-sung would no longer be in command of the army and was replaced by Chinese General Peng Dehuai as Field Commander. Over the next few years, the war was fought above and below the 38th parallel. But overall, there was little advancement. Kim Il-sung expected after losing 250,000 troops that he would have taken South Korea.. In the end, the Soviets refused to send troops into North Korea, but did supply air support, military equipment and military advisers.

A loss to American and UN forces in Korea was not an option for China. Even though the Chinese troops did not have suitable cold weather clothing, the Chinese commanders pushed deep into North Korea, thus once again out-running their resupply line. The Chinese suffered huge losses as a result. The Chinese out-numbered the UN forces by 5 to 1, but most of the casualties were due to frost bite, in which entire regiments on both sides were unable to fight due to the cold weather.

Kim Il-Sung put pressure on Stalin to provide air support, but Stalin would only agree to supply air support around the border of China and North Korea, from air bases in China only. It would later be called "Mig Alley". The American air force had free reign to bomb North Korea as long as they did not cross into "Mig Alley" air space. Without air superiority, it was hopeless for North Korea to win total victory over South Korea, so he had no choice but to negotiate an armistice on July 27, 1953.

Mac Arthur's landing at Incheon, 1951   Fig. 8

Under the terms of the armistice, North Korea gained 1,500 square miles of land near the 38th parallel. It was a heavy price to pay for North Korea and the Chinese army who suffered 365,000 casualties while the UN forces suffered 106,000 casualties.

As a result of Kim Il-sung's loss, he vowed never to trust the Soviet Union or depend on China for aid and assistance. Kim Il-sung began to build one of the largest military forces in the world, and would eventually cut all ties with the Soviet Union.

The First Juche

Kim Il-Sung was disappointed in his defeat over South Korea and decided to abandon Communism all together and create his own form of government, called a "Juche".

Kim first mentioned a Juche in 1955 and again in 1965 at an Indonesian conference. He defined a "Juche" as being independent economically and being self-reliant in managing its countries defenses. The ideology was that one man would rule the masses and would be considered the father of all the people. Like a dictator, his words and decision would go unchallenged; in exchange he would protect, feed, and provide for those who give total and complete devotion and unwavering allegiance to him. Like communism, the people would work in collectives and all aspects of manufacturing would be owned by the government, specifically by the father, who was Kim Il-sung. Another key element in the Juche government was leadership succession of the father, which would be passed down like royalty. Elections were held every five years, but only one name appeared on the ballot, which was the Father. It was compulsory for everyone of age to vote, and failure to vote meant you were not devoted to the Leader and branded as a subversive. In 1980, North Korea expanded the definition of the Juche ideology by incorporating the "Fuehrer Doctrine", which reads:

"….the Suryong (Leader or Father) is an impeccable brain of the living body, the masses can be endowed with their life in exchange for their loyalty to him, and the Party is the nerve of that living body." [52]

The doctrine allows for the cessation from father to son. The Juche Ideology is an extreme version of fascism where the leader or father of North Korea, controls the Party, similar to what Mae Zedong created in China when he ordered the Cultural Revolution and the purging of the Party Officials who were not loyal to him or his cause.

Kim Il-Sung had a cult personality, like Mao, Hitler and Mussolini. In order for Kim's system of government to work, he had to indoctrinate the people into believing he was "god" or at the very least, a descendant of god. He used propaganda in schools which began at kindergarten and lasted through college. Like all fascist and communist governments, the key was to convince the masses that they have a good life and that capitalist countries were planning to wage war against the Juche out of jealousy. His form of government was similar to a cult religion, which is based on fear and the lack of knowledge of the outside world. Isolating the masses from any outside influence was essential to the brainwashing. It followed the same format used by Mao and all other dictators, but only to a greater extreme. Censorship of radio, television, internet, books and newspaper was also part of the program of isolationism. Free assembly was prohibited, as well as any discussion about politics or criticism of the regime could bring imprisonment or death for their entire family.

Kim Il-sung's regime was unique in that he used the "carrot and stick" technique to control people. He would give gifts to party loyalist several times a year to those who performed well in manufacturing, production or farming. Large apartment complexes were built for those who were loyal and good workers of the regime. He would send purchasing agents to Europe and purchase cars, jewelry and clothing and luxury items to give to party loyalist. This was a televised event each year where expensive luxury gifts would be given away in an effort to bolster his popularity. It was like a North Korean version of Christmas. It would be televised over and over to the masses to help reinforce his loving care and humanity toward his people. It was a unique form of persuasion in which Kim used it to his advantage. Its tenants have been passed along from his grandfather, father and son, however, since the trade embargo, in a much smaller scale.

Not everything in North Korea was a "carrot". Kim used the "stick" more than he used the "carrot". Even though it's not known how many political prisoners were incarcerated in North Korean's prisons, it is estimated that thousands were sent to work. Satellite images have detected about 3 prison facilities in the North and witnesses claim that it was not a prison at all, but a work and death camp. The current leader, Kim Jong-un, did not have the charisma his father or grandfather had, so he went on a tirade and purged half his generals and party members that were appointed by his father and grandfather when they were in power. He also decided that a political prisoner should not be imprisoned, but executed, along with his entire family. He believed that a person who was disloyal to the leadership would have contaminated the minds of the rest of the family and believed that disloyalty was an inherited trait passed down from generation to generation.

After Kim Il-Sung's death in 1994, his son, Kim Jong-Il became supreme leader of North Korea until his death in 2011. His son, Kim Jong-un became the current leader of North Korea. As with all fascist and military regimes, they seldom last long. Eventually, people realized that a totalitarian government is not the utopia they envisioned. But, North Korea is much different. Their patriotism can be bought with a gold watch, an apartments or a set of dishes, because they can't buy lavish goods in North Korea. More than likely it will always be a totalitarian society, because after three generations they are not able to accept the fact that there is another world beyond North Korea. Only a few have the fortitude to escape into reality, regardless of the consequences, which could be a fate worse than death if caught. Many escape into China, but only to be returned to North Korea by the Chinese. Their fate is soon sealed along with their family.

South Korea

After World War II, it was agreed upon by the Allied powers that Korea was to be divided along the 38 parallel. Russia and the United States would administer the trusteeship of North and South Korea. It was understood from the beginning between Russia and the United States, that the division of North and South Korea would only be temporary and that they would be unified as one country as soon as both interim governments worked out the details of reunification. After repeated attempts to unify the two sides failed, the issue of reunification was given to the UN General Assembly, but North Korea rejected the proposition that a nationwide election be held to determine what kind of government the people wanted.

In 1946, North Korea wasted little time in confiscating private property as well as Japanese owned factories and businesses under state ownership. Land reform in the South had also taken place. The new government confiscated all of the Japanese held businesses and property by 1949, South Koreans who owned large land holdings were required to give up 40% to the government, but were allowed to keep the remainder for personal use and farming.

South Korea wrote a Constitution and appointed Syngman Rhee as interim president and declared on August 15, 1948, that South Korea would be called the "Republic of Korea". On September 9, 1948, Kim Il-sung called North Korea the "Democratic People's Republic of Korea. On December 12, 1948, the United Nations recognized the Republic of Korea as the sole legal government of Korea. In June of 1950, North Korea invades South Korea and after three years of bitter fighting both sides agreed to an armistice. The original border between North and South Korea had changed very little. In 1952, Rhee introduced an amendment into the Parliament which made the President an elected position. He declared martial law and arrested opposing members of

Parliament and any anti-government groups. He was elected once again as President once he eliminated all opposition.

In 1954, Rhee won another re-election, but since he held a majority in Parliament, he pushed through an amendment to the constitution which allowed him to extend the eight year term limits to indefinitely. He was re-elected again in 1956, which led to the arrest and executions of members of the opposition party. In 1956, Rhee had moved the country from democracy to a repressive dictatorship, but he still enjoyed US support during the Eisenhower Administration. When the 1960 elections were held, he easily won re-election, even though the public protested that the elections were rigged. Riots and demonstrations broke out all over South Korea, and martial law was declared. On April 26, 1960, Rhee resigned and fled into exile on a CIA, DC-4 Civil Air Transport (CAT) plane to Hawaii, where he remained until his death in 1965.

In 1960, after the fall of the Rhee regime, the Democratic Party was elected into office and made revisions to the constitution, allowing a Parliamentary Cabinet System. Yun Bo-seon was elected President and Chang Myon as Prime Minister. The new administration immediately purged those with loyalties to Rhee in the military, government and police. More than 6,200 were purged. By May of 1961, the military staged a coup d'état led by Major General Park Chung-hee. He returned the government back to the original Presidential System. In 1963, Park Chung-hee ran for President and easily won the Presidency, and over the next 18 years, his military rule would squash demonstrations and jailed hundreds of dissidents who opposed his style of military rule. His rule would end in 1979, when his own Korean Central Intelligence Agency Director (KCIA) assassinated Park Chung-hee. Prime Minister Choi Kyu-hah became

President. His Presidency would only last 6 days when General Chun Doo-hwan staged another Coup d'état.

In June of 1987, more than a million people demonstrated demanding that South Korea return to a constitutional government and a democracy. Direct elections were held for President in December of 1987, which ended the last of the military Junta's in South Korea. Roh Tae-woo became the first elected President in 16 years. South Korea remains a democratic nation ever since.

South Korea and Japan has become an economic and industrial giant in Asia in recent history, but is under constant threat from North Korea who is only miles away from its capital, Seoul and striking distance from Japan.

Chapter 7

Vietnam: The Asian Tiger

The Vietnamese are descendants of the nomadic Mongols of China and migrants from Indonesia. The country was called Nam Viet, and was ruled by China from 111 BC to the 15th century. Vietnam was originally three countries; Cochin-China, Annam and Tonkin until 1887, when France unified all three by appointing a single Governor-General which remained until Vietnam's independence in 1954.

North Vietnam's ultimate goal was to reunited with South Vietnam after the French declared Vietnam's independence in 1954. During the Geneva Conference of 1954, the United States was reluctant to get involved in Vietnam and abstained from voting to divide Vietnam into a North and South. The US position at the time was to unify the North and South Vietnam and allow the people to decide in an open election. The Geneva Convention of 1954 would change the goal of unification when the Convention voted to separated Vietnam into two separate countries, a disappointment for both North Vietnam and the United States.

The Vietnam War started over a hypothetical assumption called the "domino effect", in which each country in Asia would gradually be consumed by communist regimes. President Eisenhower, Kennedy, Johnson and Nixon reiterated the dangers of allowing Vietnam to fall to the communist in an effort to garner public support for a possible war in Asia. President John F. Kennedy sent 16,000 military advisers to Vietnam in 1962 to assist the South Vietnamese military in combating communist insurgents that infiltrated from the North, and eradicate the communist guerrillas already in the South, known as Viet Cong (VC). But even before that, Kennedy was deeply concerned about Laos and the communist North Vietnam attempting to take-over the government of Laos, which will be discussed later. After President Kennedy's death in November of 1963, Lyndon B. Johnson became President and supported much of Kennedy's programs except using direct armed conflict against the communist by using American forces on the ground in both Vietnam and Laos. This was partly due to the mock war games conducted by the Pentagon in early 1962, which predicted the out-come of a war in Southeast Asia.

The War Games

In February of 1962, nine months before the death of President Kennedy, war games were being planned in the basement of the Pentagon. A massive computer sat in large room for the purpose of strategizing a theoretical war in Southeast Asia. As events were unfolding in Laos and North and South Vietnam, the Rand Corporation was commissioned by the Pentagon to build and design a computer system that would predict the out-come of war when multiple variables were input by a group of 35 to 50 military strategist and political policy makers and advisors. The Sigma I system, was designed and built by three branches of the military. Its principal sponsor was the U.S. Air Force. The games would be conducted over a seven day period which would represent a 10 year war period. It was highly top secret and would finally be declassified after 40 years.

Sigma I-62 war games was conducted in February of 1962, in which the blue team represented the United

States, the red team; North Vietnamese communist; the yellow team, China; the brown team; South Vietnam; the black team the Viet Cong guerrillas and the green team, USSR. The games were supervised by a control team under McGeorge Bundy and umpired by General Maxwell Taylor. After seven days of a mock war game, the conclusion was that American intervention in Vietnam would be unsuccessful and South Vietnam would fall to the communist. *[Staff, pg C-34, 11/15/2014, Ball, Pgs 92-93]*

Some military officials suggested that the results were not realistic and flawed, so another War Game was conducted in the spring of 1963, and yet another in 1964, both using a revised program called Sigma II. Sigma II-63 war game predicted that the U.S. would commit 500,000 to 600,000 service men in Vietnam in which the war would last until 1970, with a loss to America and a win for the North Vietnam. Another war game in 1964, II-64, concluded that once again the U.S. would lose and as a result, Laos, Cambodia would fall to the communist as well. U.S. Air Force General Curtis Lemay, was out-raged at the results and claimed it did not take into account the massive aerial bombing of North Vietnam which would turn the tide of the war and force North Vietnam to sue for peace. Secretary of Defense Robert McNamara and General Maxwell Taylor insisted the war would be over by 1965, rather than the predicted year of 1970 by Sigma I-63.

Another war game, Sigma II-65, ended in August of 1965, in which the results indicated that the war would continue with heavy American war casualties which would frustrate the American public and demand a pull-out of the war. Sigma II-65's final conclusion was much the same as all other prior war games, which included Curtis Lemay's scenario of massive B52 bombing of the North which would have little effect on the outcome of war. It concluded that as long as the communist were engaged in a guerilla tactic, they could find refuge in Cambodia and Laos and continue raids and the war. The bombing campaigns, such as Operation Rolling Thunder and Operation Barrel Roll, by the Air Force, would have little effect on communist operations. It also advised that General Westmoreland's strategy of attrition of the enemy would not win the war.

The war games predicted an American loss and the fall of Southeast Asia to communism, contrary to Pentagon military opinion. Subsequent war games were held in 1966, 1967 and 1968, in which the impetus of the war games changed from winning the war, to inflicting damage to the north and forcing the North Vietnamese to negotiate a peace settlement favorable to the United States. As the war continued, extensive bombing failed to stop the communist insurgency in Laos and Vietnam, much of its failure was due to another war phenomena called "Rules of Engagement" (discussed later) in which only the U.S. would adhere too and the communist took advantage of. In lieu of the consistent war game results, the US continued to send the 550,000 troops and the bombing of North Vietnam as predicted in the 1963 war game.

Ho Chi Minh

Ho Chi Minh was born in May of 1890 with the given name of Nguyen Sinh Cung in central Vietnam during the period of French colonization. He worked on a steamer as a cook and traveled around the world and would settle in Paris, France in 1919. He was inspired by Lenin's Bolshevik Revolution in 1917 and joined the French Communist Party. In the 1930's he became a representative of the International Communist Organization which furthered his education toward communism. He changed his name to Ho Chi Minh in 1940, which means; "Bringer of Light". He returned to Vietnam in 1941 and traveled to China to seek support for his communist movement in Vietnam, but was arrested and imprisoned for 18 months by Chiang Kai Shek. He later returned to Vietnam and organized the Communist Party of Vietnam.

In 1949, the French returned to Indochina after the war and appointed Emperor Bao Dai as the puppet leader of Vietnam under French colonial rule, but shortly after, guerrilla fighting broke out between the French and the Communist guerrillas. In the North, the communist guerrillas were led by Ho Chi Minh's long time friend General Vo Nguyen Giap. After the fall of Dien Bien Phu, the French pulled out of Indochina in which the Geneva Convention of 1954 separated Vietnam at the 17th parallel. Ho Chi Minh would become President and a Politburo and Central Committee would be formed in North Vietnam.

Unlike other socialist and dictators, Ho Chi Minh had a connection with the 20 million people of North Vietnam. He dressed in peasant clothes and held frequent meetings with villagers to hear their concerns. He was charismatic, diplomatic, well spoken and had a firm conviction toward communism. Ho Chi Minh would never see his goal of unification of North and South Vietnam. He died September 2, 1969 at the age of 79.

The United States supported France, but at the same time wanted France out of Indochina, and stop communist aggression. The United Stated disliked colonialism and considered it a protectionist policy that stifled trade. The same was true after World War II between India and Great Britain, thus the USA supported India's independence, at least behind White House doors.

Ho Chi Minh was sure that the Geneva Conference of 1954 would unify Vietnam as one country rather than to split Vietnam into two separate States like Korea. When it came time to vote, the United States abstained while the others voted to split Vietnam at the 17th Parallel with a demilitarized zone (DMZ) between the two. The United States was non committal during the conference of 1954, without a clear goal. The one thing America didn't want was Vietnam to be a communist state. When Vietnam failed to be unified in the 1954 Conference, it set the stage for a long and protracted guerrilla war which would last for two decades and cost the lives of 1.5 million Vietnamese and 90,000 foreign military troops, of which 58,000 were American.

After the Geneva Accords in 1954, the French moved out of Hanoi in a mass migration of anti-communist, Catholics, intellectuals, land owners and business men and women. The nationalist boarded ships in Haiphong Harbor in North Vietnam, called "Operation Passage to Freedom", for resettlement in South Vietnam. More than 1 million boarded the ships which were estimated to be more than 2 million that crossed the border into South Vietnam. The CIA reported that 52,000 pro communist from the south moved to North Vietnam. More than 35,000 communist insurgents would remain in South Vietnam and would later be called Viet Cong (VC).

After the separation of Vietnam at the 17th parallel, North Vietnam's Emperor, Bao Dai abdicated and became Emperor of South Vietnam in which he selected Ngo Dinah Diem as head of the South Vietnam Army and government administrator. Shortly after, Diem would later send Bao Dai into exile and proclaimed himself as President. While Diem was a competent leader and a strict anti-communist, he was independent and would not take advice or recommendations from the U.S. It would later become his downfall.

President Kennedy's Plan for Withdrawal

Kennedy was reluctant in sending ground troops into Vietnam, but he elected to send 16,000 military advisors and staff to South Vietnam to train and act as military advisors to the South Vietnamese Army. Previous reports indicated that they were in desperate need of training in military tactics, and military discipline. The purpose was to create an effective fighting force against communist insurgents. President Eisenhower had previously sent 800 advisors to assist President Diem to help organize his military and stop the Viet Cong assassinations against government officials which had numbered over 1,100 in 1956 alone. President Kennedy was aware of the War Game results prior to his death, so he had a good grasp of the situation in Vietnam and its chances of success, which was dim unless they could get the South Vietnam Military trained as an effective fighting force. After a year of extensive training Kennedy sent Robert McNamara and General Maxwell Taylor to South Vietnam to review the progress of the training program against the Viet Cong.

Their report was given to President Kennedy, which was somewhat sobering and disturbing. Corruption in Diem's regime and the military high command was rampant and the morale among the soldiers was low, in which the troops and officers lacked the will to fight or engage the enemy. Many combat squadrons refused to go out on patrols and those who did go on patrol refused to confront the enemy directly into combat. McNamara told the President that 50% to 60% of the weapons being used by the VC were American made, and many were being sold to the VC on the black-market. There was a lack of military leadership and discipline which invited failure. While some squadrons and platoons were exceptional, most did not have the will to fight and desertions were high.

Meetings were held in Washington between Robert McNamara, Maxwell Taylor and the Military Joint Chief of

Staff, in which Kennedy wanted to withdraw 1,000 U.S. military personnel and advisors by January 1, 1963 under a National Security letter signed by Kennedy. Further withdrawals were to be scheduled later in 1964. His goal was a complete withdrawal by 1965. However, President Kennedy would be assassinated in late November of 1963, which would leave Lyndon Johnson the task of implementing the withdrawal. The orderly withdrawal of advisors, however, would not take place as planned and the stage was set for the acceleration of the war in Vietnam as LBJ's military advisors insisted it was the only course of action in defeating the North Vietnamese.

LBJ's Limited War

President Johnson approved a highly secret covert operation named; Operation 34A in January of 1964. The purpose of the covert operation was to destroy North Vietnamese radar and radio transmitters situated along the Gulf of Tonkin. The covert operations were designed to use two high speed boats commanded by three Norwegian boat commanders and a crew of South Vietnamese commandos and sponsored and financed by the CIA. The speed boats would leave Da Nang and traveled at night, heading north toward the Gulf of Tonkin. Near the Gulf of Tonkin, were two US Navy destroyers stationed 13 miles out at sea. The USS Maddox and the USS Turner Joy, which were equipped with electronic monitoring and surveillance equipment. The commandos had performed several raids in the past and returned on the morning of August 1, 1964. After destroying a radio transmitter on an island in the gulf, they returned to DaNang. The North Vietnamese navy was on alert and thought the raiding party had originated from the two U.S. destroyers. The North Vietnam Navy sent several patrol boats to intercept the ships and fired several torpedoes at the USS Maddox. Several weeks later, both ships reported another incident in which the US Navy had sunk several North Vietnam patrol boats.

In 1964, as a result of the attack against the US Navy destroyers, President Johnson requested Congress to initiate the Gulf of Tonkin Resolution, which authorized the President to use military force against the North Vietnam as he sees fit. Although not a declaration of war, it gave the President broad discretion in the use of force against North Vietnam. From this point on, the War in Vietnam began and accelerated. In retaliation, the US aircraft carriers USS Ticonderoga and USS Constellation launched air strikes against Haiphong Harbor, destroying 25 minesweepers and patrol boats belonging to the North Vietnamese navy. The Pentagon wanted to use massive firepower to bring down the enemy in a quick and decisive attack, but North Vietnam wanted to use the war strategy of guerrilla warfare of "hit and run" pioneered by Mao Zedong in China.

America's Theory of Winning the War

America's goal in the Vietnam War was not to win the war by defeating North Vietnamese Communist, but to force the North Vietnamese Communist above the 17th parallel, as we did in the Korean War at the 38th parallel. To accomplish this goal, General Westmoreland wanted to engage the enemy by fighting a war based on attrition; by killing more of them, than they kill of us. This strategy makes sense since he was not allowed to take territory to push the communist north, and he was only allowed to fight a defensive war with the North Vietnamese, yet the Communist were completely mobile and fighting offensively. Keep in mind that General MacArthur was fired by Truman for advancing beyond the Korean DMZ and the 38th Parallel, and so it would be the case with Westmoreland should he violate LBJ's orders of containment of the North Vietnamese communist.

Westmoreland's theory was based on America having superior fire power and would kill more communist insurgents than they can replace. North Vietnam had 20 million people in 1965, and South Vietnam had 60 million, so it was reasonable to assume that the communist was able to recruit as many as 1 million combat troops and 2 million in reserve should become necessary. In contrast, North Vietnam fought the war on territory gained regardless of how many lives it took. Ho Chi Minh new that he did not need to win the battles in order to win the war, which was exactly how Mao was able to defeat the nationalist in China in 1948, who fought an overwhelming military force with superior military arms and aircraft supplied by the United States. He knew that most US soldiers were on duty for a one year tour, but his soldiers remained fighting until the war was over, regardless how long it lasted.

This was a huge advantage for the North Vietnam Army (NVA), who didn't need to train replacements every year and as a result would develop battle field experience. It had the equivalent affect of doubling their troop strength because they didn't need as many troops in reserve to replace those in the field who went home. In contrast; the 535,000 US troops in Vietnam numbered 535,000 of which only about 235,000 were combat field troops, the remainder were support personnel.

The United States assumed we would be out of Vietnam by 1965, and so the American public back home became wary when the war dragged on for another 7 years. The politicians and the military were telling the public that we were winning the war, but as the years passed, it became clear that we were no better off from when the war started. We were holding ground with the insurgents on a defensive stand point, but was unable to train the South Vietnam ARVN to do the same. The American public had no idea what the basis of measurement of winning war was or did the U.S. military.

On a military stand point and in all fairness to the military and General Westmoreland in particular, the U.S. Military was at big disadvantage from the first day of entering the war. The North Vietnamese fought an offensive war, while the U.S. fought a defensive war, with the goal of containment rather than defeating the enemy. Most military strategist agree that it is much more difficult to fight a defensive war that restricts your mobility than to fight offensive war where you have mobility and can pick the battles you can win or at the very least inflict the most damage to the enemy.

The defeat of South Vietnam had more to do with South Vietnam's lack of leadership and training than most anything. Most high level positions were filled by those with family connections in government, rather than being qualified for the job. In Asian culture this is common and considered normal and standard practice. President Diem continued to assign incompetent and untrained military leaders in positions of leadership who would seldom leave military headquarters to fight in the field. The purpose was to hand pick friends he knew would not attempt a coup détente. Other problems plagued the military such as desertions and the lack of military discipline. It improve over time, but not to a level of being an effective fighting force against NVA or the VC. American's plan of Vietnamization was to have the ARVN contain the insurgents after the US pulled-out of Vietnam, but ended up as a misguided dream.

During the course of the Vietnam War, there were several attempts to modify and help change the direction of the war. Three separate plans were devised by CIA and war strategists that would attempt to break the stronghold that the Viet Cong had in South Vietnam among the rural villagers:

1) The Hamlet Resettlement Program under President Kennedy in Feb. 1962.

2) CIA's Phoenix Program under President Johnson in 1966.

3) Vietnamization Program under President Nixon in Feb. 1969.

The Hamlet Resettlement Program (The isolation approach) was based on isolating the civilian population so they couldn't join the Viet Cong Guerrilla movement. Entire villages were relocated in well guarded hamlets (compounds), where 75 to 100 ARVN troops would guard and protect them from the Viet Cong. The Hamlets were fenced and strict curfews were enforced. It was essentially a prison for civilians. Of the 1.2 million rural villagers that were relocated, nearly 80% of those who were relocated at gun point. Needless to say, most who were relocated at gun point would later become Viet Cong and NVA supporters. So this plan actually helped the Viet Cong in their efforts to recruit. The Hamlet Program lasted only a few years during the early part of the war and was cancelled.

The next Program was the Phoenix Program (the terror and assassination approach). It was designed as a terror program where CIA sponsored death squads or assassin squads would hunt down suspected VC leaders and Cadres and kill them. (This is discussed in depth later). The CIA establishing monthly assassination quotas, like Westmoreland's war of attrition, which forced many to exaggerate how many enemy they killed in combat or by assassination in order to meet the quotas. It was also used by the South Vietnamese generals and politicians to assassinate political opposition, which was much more effective as a political tool than a military tool.

Lastly, Nixon's Vietnamization Program (the sink or swim approach to war). Its goal was to have South Vietnamese soldiers replace the US troops in combat toward the end of the war. There were a lot of reasons why this program failed, corruption within the leadership was one of the main causes of failure. It was also prevalent at all levels of the military which was demoralized the troops. Promotions were based on nepotism and who they knew in high places in government and the military. It was a formula for failure from the start. Another reason for failure was America's training program of the South Vietnam Military which was centered around fighting a conventional war (John Wayne Style), while the enemy was fighting a guerrilla war of hit and run. The South Vietnamese military should have fought the North Vietnamese as guerrilla fighters, which is what they were skilled at. What the US needed was a realistic long term battle plan from the first day the troops landed in Vietnam, and realize they were fighting a guerrilla war rather than a conventional war of attrition. General Westmoreland spent most of his time trying to get the NVA to come-out into the open and fight a conventional war, so his body count figures would show we were winning. Ho Chi Minh and General Giap on the other hand knew it was military suicide to expose their army to a superior fire power of the United States and elected to pick and choose their battles carefully, which they did.

Politically, America was fearful of exacerbating the war which would cause China to enter the conflict and provide North Vietnam millions of combat troops as they had during the Korean War. They were already supplying military equipment, guns and anti-aircraft batteries to the North in an effort to protect their supply routes from

China to Hanoi, but direct troop involvement could expand the war into China. As the war dragged on, they were forced to supply rice and food to the citizens of North Vietnam because the men had gone off to war and wasn't able to harvest rice for their families. The US was hesitant at first to bomb above the 17th parallel, especially Hanoi and Hai Pong Harbor for fear that a Chinese ship maybe docked, which could cause and international incident and draw the Chinese into the war.

After the war, the Chinese admitted that they had no intension of being embroiled into a war with the US, unless we bombed too close to the border of China, where there were large populations of indigenous Chinese. They also admitted that they believed Vietnam would win the war anyway; all that was required of them was to supply them with the arms and materials to finish the job, regardless how long it took. The US Government wasn't sure what the Chinese would do if we began bombing Hanoi, but was reasonably certain as long as the bombing was confined to the surrounding areas around Hanoi and the Ports, there would not be an escalation of the war. In the Rules of Engagement, Hanoi and Haiphong Harbor would be off limits to bombing.

During the Vietnam War, the people in the United States, including Congress, were unaware that we were bombing Laos at a rate of 1 bomb every 3 minutes. It became the most bombed country in the history of the world. More bombs landed in Laos than in Germany and England during World War II. The public had no idea that we were fighting two wars at once; Laos and Vietnam simultaneously. Perhaps America's disdain toward the war in Southeast Asia had turned sour because of the constant political deception orchestrated by the government and military by giving the American people a false sense of hope that we were winning the war by using body count as a measure of success. The one thing that remained firm in

US policy was that American troops were not allowed to invade North Vietnam above the 17th Parallel.

This was frustrating for the American troops and in many ways demoralizing, partly because the NVA had establish a large military base inside the DMZ (Demilitarized Zone) and would move troops south at night and conduct raids on US military installations, then slip back across the 17th parallel in the cover of darkness, knowing that US troops would not follow them. This hit and run tactic was also the method that the Viet Cong used in the south to disrupt and demoralize the enemy, even though it was much less effective.

General Westmoreland thought there weren't enough American ground troops in Vietnam to hold all the positions we took from the NVA. However, it would seem to me with South Vietnam's 960,000 ARVN forces, we should have been able to hold those key positions easily. After numerous battles such as Hamburger Hill, Khe San and the Rock Pile, the American's abandoned them after hundreds of lives were lost defending and taking control of an area. The NVA would move back into the area that was lost just days and weeks before. Had we adopted this strategy during World War II, we would have never defeated Germany or Japan. This had a very demoralizing effect on the American and allied troops, which made our troops wonder what they were fighting and dying for. But, American and Allied troops were never told that the goal was not to defeat the enemy and take territory but rather kill enough Vietnamese until they were willing to negotiate peace and promise to remain above the 17th parallel, as per the Geneva Accords of 1954.

US troops became disgruntled and demoralized after years of fighting, and many turned to drugs. By the end 1960, Thirty thousand American troops in Vietnam were addicted to heroin. Combat solders were dying of drug overdose at a rate of two per day. Much of the drug trafficking was tracked back to officials within the South Vietnam government and the Golden Triangle in Burma and Laos, as the main source.

North Vietnam's Theory of Winning the War

In contrast, Ho Chi Minh and General Giap used the Chinese method of revolutionary war tactics pioneered by Mao Zedong in his book "Guerrilla Warfare". China and the Soviet Union supplied 600 military advisors to assist North Vietnam. Like the 16,000 advisors supplied by the United States in the South, the advisors trained the troops on the use of equipment and served as observers and let the NVA to do the fighting, whereas American advisors trained the troops on all aspects of military training . The military operation was entirely run by the Politburo and Central Committee, which was headed by Ho Chi Minh. General Giap had complete control of the military operations with little interference from the Politburo and with little restraints. The Viet Cong and the NVA operated offensively throughout the war, rather than defensive like the United States and South Vietnam. It would be their major war strategy which would prove successful throughout the nine years of war.

During the 1954 and 1962 Geneva Conventions; Laos and Cambodia declared neutrality, however, North Vietnam had no intention of moving communist insurgents and troops out of South Vietnam. They knew the Geneva Agreement would not be enforced. The United States was aware that the North Vietnam was violating the Geneva Convention, but was unable to enforce the terms of the agreement. This was a reoccurring theme used by communist and in particular North Vietnam. Agreements meant little or nothing to the North Vietnamese as long as it gave them an advantage, which was Mao Zedong's theory of guerrilla warfare he outlined in his book. Which played perfectly into Ho Chi Minh's plan.

On a military strategy stand point, when the French pulled-out of Indochina in 1954, North Vietnam had already established a large military contingent in the south. Perhaps as many as 130,000 communist troops remained in the South and took the role as Viet Cong guerrillas.

There was continued political instability in South Vietnam; much of it was stirred-up by communist insurgents which was their purpose. After Thieu took office, many rural villagers continued to support the Viet Cong. The military tactic of hit and run by the VC rendered American's combat techniques ineffective when fighting a guerrilla war. Westmoreland tried every technique to get the guerrilla's to fight head on, but only on several occasions would they engage and only briefly and would vanish back into the jungle without notice. The theory of containment was clearly not working in Vietnam, and the US Government did little to change its strategy. Some of the proposals offered by Westmoreland were rejected in Washington, so he was left with the same political war during his term as Commanding General.

Even though the US military won every major battle in South Vietnam, the Chinese and Ho Chi Minh knew that the US would lose South Vietnam to the communist. America was obsessed with battle field casualties and General Giap was not. General Giap used suicide squads to charge military positions with bombs strapped to their waist; much like the Kamikaze's in World War II. In all fairness to General Westmoreland leadership, he did his best he under the political restraints he had to work with. Many of his plans were "shot down" by President Johnson and the Military Chief of Staff who were rigid in their belief that containment could be achieved in South

Vietnam and win the war.

Rules of Engagement

Every country and every war in Asia had separate rules of engagement with the enemy. Rules of Engagement started with the Korean War for fear that China and the Soviet Union would get involved in the war. In Vietnam the ROE were somewhat the same as Korea only much more encompassing. One set of rules applied to Laos, another for North Vietnam and yet another for Cambodia. Rules of engagement (ROE) were changed from time-to-time depending on the political atmosphere or who the President was at the time. ROE's were written by political staff and analyst close to the President. In contrast, Laws of War (LOW) were established at The Hague Convention of 1899 and 1907 that covered 1) Laws of War 2) War Crimes and 3) International Law. The Rules of Engagement created during the Korean and Vietnam War was an effort to avoid expanding the war in Asia, but since ROE were political, they were also classified and considered secret. There were two reasons why they were classified;

1) They didn't want the enemy to know the areas or targets that were off-limits to bombing and certain combat conditions for ground troop deployment while being engaged with the enemy.
2) They wanted to keep the information secret from the public and media for political reasons.

However, they did manage to keep ROE's secret from the public for more than 40 years; however, the North Vietnamese leadership was well aware of the rules of engagement perhaps only days or weeks after they were implemented. It is not known how they knew, but they were able to take advantage of the political situation to their advantage. The Raven Squadron was being operated by the CIA as Air America and Continental Air Services in Laos which was authorized by the President Kennedy in 1961. The Raven Squadron, which was made up of military pilots that didn't really get deployed into Laos until 1967, but civilian pilots were contracted by the CIA from the beginning to transport men and equipment to areas of battle. Its purpose was to provide air support to the Meo ground troops fighting the communist insurgents in Laos. General Vang Pao and the pilots raised concerns that the ROE's were restricting their ability to fight effectively in an effort to stop or slow-down the communist insurgents from North Vietnam. Maps were given to the Raven pilots which marked the locations of areas not to be bombed. Off limits to bombing included; towns and villages, radio towers, hospitals, temples and a 10 mile corridor along the Laos and Chinese border, and the Laos-Vietnam border. A road system was being constructed by the Chinese from the border into Laos and another road being constructed by Vietnam from Hanoi into Laos for the purpose of transporting military equipment and troops, which would connect the two road systems. The roads were also considered off limits to bombing while under construction, for reasons unknown.

Ho Chi Minh Trail was also off limits to bombing for the most part, since Laos and Cambodia announced their neutrality, however, the Raven Squadron in Laos bombed the trail since they weren't an officially a military organization, at least openly. They were not allowed to bomb surface to air missile sites (SAM) if they were under construction and the pilot was not in imminent danger or threat of being fired upon. North Vietnam also had similar restrictions in place that included certain power plants, dams and dikes and certain bridges that were not to cause undue hardship on the civilian population.

A ten mile free zone existed around Hanoi and Haiphong Harbor as well as the demilitarize zone (DMZ) where the North Vietnam was using as a combat staging area. Other areas included large tracks of forested land and a 10 mile corridor on the Chinese-Vietnamese border. The Vietnamese of course installed SAM sites inside the city of Hanoi and on dikes, dams and bridges and temples that were declared free zones under the ROE. This in effect rendered the bombing of North Vietnam and Laos almost ineffective on a standpoint of destroying North Vietnams infrastructure and military targets. This fact was well established in the War Games, in which the conclusion was that the heavy bombing of "Operation Rolling Thunder" and "Operation Barrel Roll" would have little effect on the out-come of the war overall. It would slow the advance of the communist invasion but wouldn't stop it.

Some say that the ROE was the major reason why America lost the war in Vietnam, but in retrospect, the first war game Sigma I-62, didn't include massive aerial bombing of North Vietnam as part of the war strategy, but the subsequent games included a massive aerial bombing campaign of North Vietnam in which Air Force General Curtis LeMay insisted that aerial bombing would win the war. The results were slightly better, but overall results were the same. The ROE had more of a demoralizing effect on American pilots for which the war games couldn't measure.

The Pentagon and the Joint Chief of Staff were insistent that massive bombing was the only way to win the war and force a peace agreement. When in November of 1967, Secretary of Defense, Robert McNamara, (who was party to the war games) sent President Johnson a memo recommending freeze troop levels, stop bombing

North Vietnam and turn-over all ground fighting to the South Vietnamese. President Johnson did not reply back, and McNamara was given the cold shoulder by Johnson and the Chief of Staff.

A1 Sky raider drops 500 lb. bombs in 1964 Fig 8a

Defense Secretary, Robert McNamara and LBJ both were sure the war would be over by 1965, LBJ was convinced by his military advisors that a win in Vietnam was obtainable; even though he had doubts but blindly followed their advice. Shortly after, Robert McNamara would resign after seven year as Secretary of Defense.

Ngo Dinah Diem's Regime

After the 1954 Geneva Accords, the United States became the political "go between" for South Vietnam. Ngo Dinah Diem who became Prime Minister of South Vietnam in the mid 1950's and would later self appoint himself President. He was educated in Hanoi as a lawyer at a French University and was a practicing Catholic when the Geneva Accords were signed in 1954, Diem moved to

South Vietnam and started his political Career as Prime Minister and President of South Vietnam. He refused to hold national elections as promised when he was appointed Prime Minister, but under pressure from the United States, in 1959, he reluctantly agreed to hold elections. His opponent was Phan Quang Dan, who was critical of Diem's government as being excessive and opulent and corrupt. Phan Quang Dan easily won the election by a 6 to 1 margin but was arrested by Diem on a variety of made up charges. In 1956, the last French soldiers moved out of Saigon and North Vietnam wasted little time in violating the peace agreement by not moving the Viet Minh soldiers stationed in the South back into North Vietnam, as stipulated in the Geneva Agreement. **[Footnote 7]**

They also began a massive military build-up of forces in the north, which was supplied by China and the Soviet Union. While the military build-up continued, Diem's government was reducing the size of its military force by half. This opened the door for increased guerrilla activity in the South.

The United States moved military advisors into South Vietnam under the Kennedy Administration, but the State Department and the US Ambassador to Vietnam, Henry Cabot Lodge Jr, was becoming frustrated with Diem's corruption and nepotism in his government. To offset his military incompetence, Diem had a deep rooted hatred for the Communist, partly because being Catholic and his brother being buried alive by the Viet Minh shortly after the Geneva Peace Accords of 1954, and wanted revenge. While he ruled the South, he banned all brothels and opium dens and even enacted a law that disallowed divorces, in keeping with the Catholic religious doctrine in a country were 80% Buddhist, which attributed to the formula for failure.

Diem was paranoid of being over thrown, and created a secret police similar to the SS of Nazi Germany. He spent more time and money chasing anti Diem supporters than he did fighting the Viet Cong. He assigned his family to Ambassadorships in Great Britain and United States and his brother to operate his secret police.

In 1963, the political atmosphere between the United States and Diem's government had completely broken down. Diem had appointed his youngest brother, Ngo Dinh Nhu as the commander of the South Vietnam Special Forces (ARVN), which was in fact Diem's secret police force. His military generals were appointed not based on their military skill but rather their connection to the Diem's regime. In 1959, Nhu orchestrated a failed assignation attempt on Cambodian Prince Sihanouk by sending him a letter bomb which further created hostilities between South Vietnam and Cambodia.

Relations with Cambodia became strained and Nhu relied on force rather than diplomacy to solve grievances and vendettas. His abuse of power didn't stop there. The Buddhist staged uprisings, claiming that the pro-Catholic Regime was trying to destroy the Buddhist religion in South Vietnam and replacing it with Catholicism. Nhu used his special forces to raid temples and arrested more than 400 monks while killing hundreds during the attacks. As the Buddhist crisis began to spread throughout South Vietnam, by August of 1963, General Le Van Kim and General Duong Van Minh of the ARVN Special Forces asked US Ambassador, Henry Cabot Lodge Jr. "if a coup was staged against Diem Regime, would the United States object?" The United States assured them that they would not interfere or get involved into domestic politics. CIA operative, Lucien Conein, gave $42,000 to a group of South Vietnamese Generals to assist in the coup d'état and with the assurance that the USA would not give Diem "safe harbor" to him or his family. [23] [24]

With the assurances from the US Government and the CIA and US Ambassador to Vietnam, Henry Cabot Lodge Jr., the rebel forces stormed the Palace, only to find that Diem and Nhu had escaped through a secret tunnel.

Diem and Nhu were aware of the plot, and escape to a Catholic Church in Cholon, a short distance from Saigon. They remained in contact with the rebels while in the shelter, hoping to negotiate a deal in exchange for their surrender. They insisted on a safe exile, possibly to the Philippines, which was a protectorate of the United States. The rebels agreed to their demands of safe passage if they surrendered. Hours later, Nhu and Diem surrendered to the ARVN.

After Diem and Nhu surrender, Diem called the US Ambassador, Henry Cabot Lodge Jr. by phone in which Lodge put Dim on hold for a lengthy period of time contemplating Diem's fate, and told him he would give them asylum to the Philippines, but it would take at least one day to make the arrangements for a plane. Colonel Mike Dunn who was the Ambassador's aid, suggested that he escort them, so that they would not be killed or harmed, but Lodge replied, "We just can't get involved". Later that day on November 2, 1963, their bodies were found at the entrance of the Catholic Church where they were hiding. Colonel Dunn asked Ambassador Lodge, why he didn't do more to save them, he replied, "What would we have done if they had lived? Every Colonel in the world would made use of them." [22]

There was a U.S. Senate Investigation in the early 1970's, to determine why Ambassador Lodge put Diem on hold for a lengthy period of time before offering him asylum. The U.S. Government didn't want to arrange a flight from Saigon to take Diem and Nhu out of the country because it would implicate the U.S. in the conspiracy, especially after guaranteeing that the U.S.

Government would not get involved in the Coup. When Ho Chi Minh heard of the assassination of Diem, he replied,

"I can scarcely believe the Americans would be so stupid."

The North Vietnamese Politburo said; it will cause more coup d'état in the future. [22]

"The consequences of the 1 November Coup d'état will be contrary to the calculations of the U.S. imperialists...Diem was one of the strongest individuals resisting the people and Communism. Everything that could be done in and attempt to crush the revolution was carried out by Diem ....The coup d'état on 1 November 1963 will not be the last." [22]

Ho Chi Minh and the Politburo were vocal and surprised of the assassination of President Diem and Nhu, but in reality they shouldn't be too surprised, since Ho Chi Minh and his Cadres ordered more than 1,100 assassinations in 1956 against President Diem's political supporters and government officials after his election. North Vietnam did more to destabilize the South Vietnam government for their own benefit than any other cause or group.

Viet Cong Terrorism

During the early part of the war, before US troops landed in South Vietnam in 1965, South Vietnam was in a political crisis. Diem and Nhu had been assassinated and a new government was in transition. The VC wanted to create more chaos by using terrorism with the hope that the South Vietnam government would collapse. In 1964 alone, 436 government officials were murdered and 161 were wounded as a result of attempts on their lives. Another 1,131 were abducted and assumed murdered. These forms of terrorism continue through much of the war. The terrorist activities by the Viet Cong went back to 1956, when 1,100 government officials and political leaders were assassinated in a single year. It is not known how many were killed by kidnapping and murder, but it is assumed to be in the thousands over the course of the war. It also illustrates the depth North Vietnam was willing to go to win the war.

Nguyen Khanh was a three star military general in the South Vietnam's Army when he orchestrated a Coup against President Duong Van Minh in January 1964. He made some effort to connect with the people and created the High National Council (HNC) at the request of the United States to get civilians involved in the political process which would stabilize the political factions that had been alienated by the military regimes in the past. But shortly after taking power he disbanded the HNC and returned to the same military strong arm of government.

As a result, demonstrations continued through the summer and winter of 1964. Retired General Maxwell Taylor replaced Henry Cabot Lodge Jr. as US Ambassador to Vietnam and in June of 1964, Maxwell Taylor requested a meeting with the South Vietnam's Armed Forces Council and recommended they stop the military in-fighting and improve South Vietnam's military efficiency and direct their attention toward fighting communist insurgents. President Johnson threatened to pull all US aid to South Vietnam and pull-out unless the situation improved drastically. However, the political chaos in South Vietnam continued against Khanh's Regime, until February 16, 1965, when the Armed Forces Council staged yet another coup détente and removed Khanh, and installed a civilian, Dr. Phan Huy Quat as Prime Minister, however, he became so frustrated with government and resigned only after a few months in office. The Military Council installed Air Marshal Nguyen Cao Ky as Prime Minister.

Nguyen Van Theiu's Regime

119

Thieu became President of South Vietnam in 1967, and Ky appointed Prime Minister, while the TET Offensive was being planned by North Vietnam. He was a devoted General of South Vietnam, however, once elected President, political rallies and demonstrations became more frequent. He had been accused of being a drug lord with direct connections with the Laos military in the drug trade. After the TET Offensive began he imprisoned his political opponents, much like Diem had. He shut down the newspaper, TV news and free assembly. He was called the "little dictator" by the people who elected him in office. He became worrisome to the United States who supported him and Nguyen Cao Ky. Even though he had a sincere desire to defeat the communist, he lacked the military knowledge to accomplish the goal.

The War in Vietnam entered into peace talks in 1969. Nixon realized that a victory in Vietnam was unobtainable. Lyndon Johnson had finally accepted the fact that Vietnam would be a loss and would not seek re-election. In reality he relied heavily on his military advisors opinions of winning the war rather than seeing the handwriting on the wall, which was perhaps the main reason why he did not accept the Democratic nomination for a second term as President. Nixon wanted to negotiate a "peace with honor" in keeping with his campaign promise of ending the Vietnam War.

Nixon assured Theiu that any violation of the Paris Peace Agreement of 1973 by North Vietnam, the United States would return and continue bombing Hanoi. Hanoi was off-limits to bombing under the ROE, but would bomb North Vietnam areas no listed in the ROE. He also assured Theiu that the United States would supply military aid after the US troops pulled-out so that he would not be "holding the bag". However, Nixon resigned in August of 1974 as a result of the Watergate scandal and the new administration under Gerald Ford appropriated

$700 million in military aid along with Australia's $300 million to Vietnam, however the Case-Church Amendment passed by Congress discontinued the bombing of Vietnam, Cambodia and Laos, effective August 16, 1973, unless congress grants approval. It is not certain where the one billion dollars per year was spent, but it is certain most didn't go toward the military to fight insurgents.

Theiu became very vocal about being betrayed by the United States, claiming America "threw him under the bus" by not supplying military aid, but that was not true. Theiu was just another dictator who may have diverted military funds elsewhere. Theiu was accused of accepting 3 million British pounds in bribes if he accepted the peace agreement, which he did. His wife was accused of confiscating 700 acres of land illegally. When South Vietnam fell, he fled to England in obscurity and later moved to Boston, Massachusetts where he died in 2001. It was later revealed that when Theiu fled South Vietnam in April of 1975, and his administration was "riddled" with communist spies. Even his closest confidants were later found to be communist infiltrators. The 3 million pound bribe could be called his severance pay. It is not known who paid the bribe, but it wouldn't be much of a stretch to assume that the U.S. Government may have been involved.

Ho Chi Minh Trail

If there was one single military tactic that sealed the fate of America in the war; the Ho Chi Minh Trail. The TET offensive certainly turned the American public against the war even though it was a military failure, but even the TET offensive couldn't have happened without the well organized and coordinated effort by the North Vietnamese in developing and maintaining a 1,200 mile supply route called the Ho Chi Minh Trail and the Sihanouk Trail from

Cambodia. The Ho Chi Minh Trail was opened for operation in 1959 as a foot path from North Vietnam to the central highlands of South Vietnam. Several years later, it was expanded to accommodate trucks and heavy equipment with numerous off-shoots to key fortifications along the Cambodian border. The North Vietnamese Army, (NVA), only had the overland route but the trail would link up to the Sihanouk Trail from the port in Cambodia. Most often, the Vietnamese moved supplies either on the backs of the North Vietnamese or by truck transport down the Ho Chi Minh Trail and Sihanouk Trail into Laos and Cambodia, weather permitting.

The Ho Chi Minh Trail was named by the Americans during early part of the war, for the large network of trails and roads that meandered along the border of Vietnam and Laos and Cambodia.

This network allowed supplies to be transported overland to the Viet Cong (VC) in the south and later the NVA. The job of maintaining the network fell upon a group known as Doan 559, Transportation Division of North Vietnam. More than 40,000 worked on the network with another 60,000 as a support team that included mechanics, hospital staff, camp personnel and maintenance crews. North Vietnamese women and children who worked on the trail were paid $1.50 per month.

Laotians and prisoners of war also worked on the trail. The Ho Chi Minh trail had been bombed many times, but was easily repaired even after an intense bombing raid. The NVA established dummy or false routes to confuse the pilots of the actual active location of the trail. Anti-defoliant, called Agent Orange was used with limited results, and did little to slow down the movement of troops and military weapons heading south. There were so many trails and off shoots, it was nearly impossible to determine which route to bomb and which route NVA would be using from one day to the next.

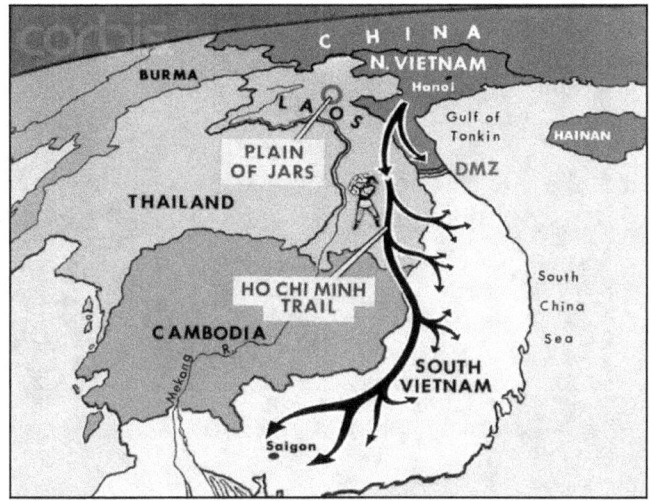

Ho Chi Minh Trail Fig. 9

For the most part, the American command decided it would be best to bomb the trail at night when the NVA convoys were forced to use lights when moving large convoys or troops down the trail. Often times, North Vietnamese, women, children and troops would backpack weapons and supplies using oil lanterns that stretched for miles and could be seen by American aircraft pilots returning to their bases after a bombing mission in the North. The Americans sent reconnaissance aircraft and drop flares on the trail when they spotted a lit convoy moving south. About 20 to 30 minutes later, the fighter bombers would arrive and drop bombs on the trail where the convoy once were. By the time the bombers arrived, the convoy would be 3 or 4 miles down the trail, hiding in the jungle with lights off.

The Ho Chi Minh Trail, T-54 Russian tanks, 1972 Fig. 9B
Courtesy of Luong Nghia/Patrick Chauvel Foundation Fig 9B

Maintenance camps and crews were stationed along the trail ready to repair sections which were destroyed by bombs. Even though there were massive bombing raids on the Ho Chi Minh Trail, the effectiveness was perhaps only 20%, which only slowed the supply train but never completely stopped it. Even Ho Chi Minh acknowledged before his death in 1969 that had the US cut off the supplies from the Ho Chi Minh Trail, they would have been defeated.

The US made an all-out effort to try to destroy the supply routes by air but was forbidden to take ground troops into Laos and Cambodia during most of the early part of the war, because of their declared neutrality at the Geneva Convention in 1962 with Cambodia and Laos.

When the US Air Force started bombing the Ho Chi Minh Trail in the mid 1960's, they would "Sheep Dip" the planes before bombing raids into Laos and Cambodia.

"Sheep Dip" was a term used by the Air Force when an aircraft was completely stripped of their paint and markings and serial numbers.

Even the pilots carried no identification or military clothing. The reason being was obvious, since the US would deny being involvement in a covert operation against a country that declared its neutrality and couldn't prove its origin of the plane or its pilot. However, it was a poor political strategy since everyone knew that the United States had the only Air Force in Vietnam and Laos, targeting communist insurgents.

The TET Offensive

Throughout the early part of the 1960's, the New Year's holiday, called TET, January 31 to February 13, has always been negotiated as an armistice so the Vietnam people could enjoy the biggest holiday in Vietnam. However, the armistice has been often violated by North Vietnam on several different occasions before the TET Offensive of 1968, so it shouldn't have surprise in 1968. What surprised General Westmoreland most was the extent of the offensive and the NVA's ability to mobilize so much arms and equipment in such short notice.

The TET Offensive was the brain child of North Vietnam's Central Office for South Vietnam, General Nguyen Chi Thanh. In 1967, he proposed a massive offensive in South Vietnam whose purpose was to turn the South Vietnam into a state chaos in which the South Vietnamese would stage an uprising against the South Vietnamese government and revolt and overthrow the unpopular government of Thieu and Ky. There had been numerous anti-war demonstrations in Saigon at the time and General Thanh believed a massive invasion would spark a revolt which would cause the overthrow of Thieu's government. He also felt that the South Vietnamese army was not an effective fighting force capable to stopping an invasion. The offensive would involve an attack against 64 district capitals and 155 attacks on air fields, government headquarters and military bases in the south. When his proposal was received by the Politburo, the Military Central Commission requested General Thanh to present his proposal in person on July 6, 1967 in Hanoi.

After presenting his proposal, he went to a party, got drunk and died of a heart attack. General Giap, was the Defense Minister, and didn't plan or command any portion of the offensive and left the details to General Tran Van Tra, who replaced General Thanh after his death. In October of 1967, it was decided that the invasion would commence on Vietnam's biggest holiday, TET, which began on the full moon of January 30, 1968.

I won't belabor the reader with details of the TET Offensive, but discuss the political aspects. The TET Offensive involved a force of 323,000 NVA and VC. During the summer of 1967, U.S. Intelligence reported a large increase in convoys' activity traveling the Ho Chi Minh Trail from the usual 480 per month to 6,316 by December of 1967. The US Military Command was certain that something big was being planned but had no idea what. Border clashes sprang-up all along the Laos and Cambodia border in December and mid January, to draw U.S. military forces away from the cities to the border areas of South Vietnam. When the TET Offensive began on January 30th, it came as a surprise to everyone, except the North Vietnamese. There were actually 3 phases of the TET Offensive which lasted until September of 1968. The first phase of the offensive was the main thrust which lasted until the City of Hue was liberated in March. Over-all, the TET Offensive was a big failure for the North Vietnamese, other than being shown on nightly news in America. The American public was getting weary of the war and was beginning to question if we were really winning the war as President Johnson and General Westmoreland often claimed. Westmoreland would be replaced by General Abrams shortly after the TET offensive, in which the policy toward the war would drastically change.

For the North Vietriam, it didn't get the desired results it expected. The South Vietnamese still supported their government and no overthrow took place as planned. However, in the rural countryside, the Viet Cong did gathered more support, but not enough to off-set the 181,000 Viet Cong killed during the year of 1968. After 1968, more and more NVA were seen in the South as a result of the heavy losses of the Viet Cong, in which they would replaced with NVA.

During the TET offensive, 4,124 Americans and Allies were killed, while South Vietnam lost 4,954. For the North Vietnamese, it is estimated that not less than 45,000 were kill and an unknown number of Viet Cong, perhaps as many as 80,000 may have been killed.

The Massacre at Hue

Perhaps the longest and heaviest battle during the Vietnam War was the Battle of Hue (Way). During the TET offensive in early March of 1968, the North Vietnamese and Viet Cong invaded the City of 140,00, which was seventeen miles south of the DMZ. The NVA took control of the entire city during the week of the TET Holiday. The city was protected by a garrison of South Vietnamese troops who had headquarters in the ancient citadel inside the city. The US Navy had a small Naval supply facility in Hue in which war ships were anchored in the gulf. There was a small air base about 10 miles from Hue with a small detachment of Marines. The North Vietnamese were well aware that Hue was lightly defended, which made it an easy target for the 10 battalions of NVA to take control of the city. Although the NVA was able to hold Hue for four weeks before US forces were able drive them out, it became the bloodiest fighting of the war. American and ARVAN troops went house to house and destroying almost the entire city in the process. The siege of Hue was over within twenty-one days once 15 battalions arrived to assist in liberating the city.

During the four weeks of North Vietnamese occupation, the North Vietnamese controlled the city, they assumed they would be able to hold the city indefinitely. They began to systematically purge the civilian population almost immediately. Months before the invasion, VC secretly collected the names of all those whom they believed were pro nationalist, which included civilian, military, Catholics, monks and government leaders. Once the NVA seized the city, they were marched to a prison camp outside of the city, but when it became clear that the NVA were losing the battle of Hue, they executed all of the prisoners. It was estimated that 4,756 were executed by the NVA during the siege of Hue and another 1,900 were listed as missing. [75]

My Lai Massacre

American troops were not immune from war atrocities either. The My Lei Massacre, also known as "Pinkville" by the military, wasn't the only incident of atrocities in South Vietnam of civilians by either side. Other soldiers have come forward claiming that civilian massacres by US troops occurred from 1968 to 1969, in order to come-up with the body count quota or in some rare cases a rogue soldier going crazy. The My Lei Massacre occurred in the small villages of My Lai and My Khe, near the village of Son My on March 16, 1968. The CIA Intelligence reports claimed that the region was a base for the Viet Cong. The American soldiers of Company 'C' of Task Force Barker were ordered by Capt. Ernest L. Medina to advance to the villages and burn and destroy the village of My Lei and kill all Viet Cong. Military reports indicated that the 48th Viet Cong Battalion was using My Lai as a staging area, however, as it turned out, their intelligence report may have been completely incorrect.

When Company 'C' field commander Lt. William L. Calley with 105 soldiers arrived at the village of My Lei and My Khe, about 350 old men, women and children were living in the village. The Viet Cong, had fled early in the morning and Lt. Calley ordered his men to round-up all civilian villagers and move them to a ditch along the road. He then ordered his troops to burn the village, but something triggered a chain reaction of murder and rape of the entire village of civilians as well as the village of My Khe nearby. Lt. Calley was accused of allowing atrocities to continue, and did little to stop it. Some soldiers testified he ordered the death of all villagers. Lt. Calley claimed he was only following orders that Capt. Ernest L. Medina issued. Capt. Medina maintained he also was following orders that were passed down to him. Somewhere, there was a serious miscommunication in the command.

The massacre ended when a helicopter landed, and a pilot, Warrant Officer Hugh Thompson, confronted Lt. Calley and demanded he stop the carnage. Thompson and his crew took some survivors in his helicopter in order to spare their lives. The helicopter had a photographer on board, Ron Haeberle, who took photos of the massacre while Thompson was trying to get Calley to stop the murders. Three other soldiers in Company 'C' tried to shield themselves over the villagers to avoid them from being shot. Later the three soldiers would get death threats if they ever told anyone of the massacre. It is not known for certain how many were killed and how many had been raped, but the military claimed that 347 deaths while the local government claimed 504 men, women and children had been murdered in My Lai and My Khe on that fateful day.

When Company 'C' arrived back in camp, rumors surfaced about the My Lai massacre. Warrant Officer Thompson reported the incident to his Commander, Colonel Henderson when he returned back to base. For more than a year, the secret of My Lai and the My Khe massacre was buried within the 11th Brigade command. The command thought of My Lei as an incident rather than a massacre. The war was already unpopular in America and it was felt that a leak about the massacre would infuriated the American public further against the Vietnam War.

On March 27, 1968, Colonel Henderson issued a letter of Commendations to Captain Medina in which a combat action report was issued on March 16, 1968 claiming that the My Lai raid was a complete success with 128 Viet Cong killed. General Westmoreland, head of the MACV, sent a congratulatory letter to Company "C", 1st Battalion, 20th Infantry for "…outstanding action … and that they dealt the enemy a heavy blow". I would assume Westmoreland had no knowledge of the massacre at that point in time and that the lower command hid the information from MACV command.

Ron Ridenhour in the 11th brigade heard about the massacre and began writing letters to President Nixon, the State Department and the Pentagon, but didn't get a reply. Finally he wrote to Seymour Hersh, who was an investigative journalist who published the story in the paper. In addition, the photographer, Ron Haeberle, shared some of his photos of the My Lai massacre with the Ohio newspaper, "Plain-Dealer" which published the photos in the November 1969 edition of the newspaper.

By this time, the military cover-up had moved to "damage control". A public enquiry was ordered. Lieutenant General Williams Peers' report of March 1970, charged 28 officers of cover-up. The Army charged only

14 with crimes; however all were acquitted except Lt. Calley. Starting in 1965, Operation Phoenix began in South Vietnam, which was a CIA program, which may have been one reason why Lt. Calley believed that murdering entire villages was acceptable. When General Peers finalized his report, a clue emerged, as to why no one was held responsible for the atrocities at My Lei and My Khe. He listed this explanation: *"perfunctory instruction in the laws of war in the U.S. Army training regime as a contributory cause of the My Lai Massacre."* [71] **[Footnote 8]**

Operation Phoenix

The Phoenix program started in South Vietnam between 1965 and 1966 by the CIA. It was highly classified program in which its purpose was to disrupt and neutralize the organizational structure of the Viet Cong, so they would not be an effective fighting guerrilla force.

By definition it sounded like a good plan and a good military strategy, but upon closer inspection the only way it could be accomplished was to neutralize all of the Viet Cong leaders and the entire Viet Cong itself, which was the goal of the war anyway.

The Purpose of the Phoenix program was to create an assassination squad to eliminate the upper command of the Viet Cong and cause chaos within the organizational command structure.

In order to accomplish the goal, it was important to know who to assassinate, so a blacklist was kept by the CIA agents who worked in the field. In 1966 and 1967, the CIA recruited 1,000 agents to collect information for the blacklist of those worthy of assassination. Most of which was to be cadres of the VC upper echelon. The Viet Cong were categorized into in one of 4 groups:

A. Party Member or Important Official

B.   Cadre in Key Position

C.   Rank and file Guerrilla, Courier, Local member

D. Villager (non combatant)

To make sure that the program remained on track, neutralization monthly goals were established. A CIA memo suggested that 1,800 VC were to be neutralized per month. [17]

However, as I will point out later in the chapter, the real goal was to kill those in groups A, B and C. In order for the project to work properly, they needed data and information about who the leaders were and their specific duties. It took several years for a team of CIA agents and Military investigators to complete a list of about 81,740 names. The next phase was the "neutralization" process, which started in late 1967 and lasted until about 1971. Of the 81,740 VC identified, 22,013 defected, 33,358 were captured and detained and 26,369 were killed. [17]

The CIA maintains that only 14% were assassinated out of the 26,369 that were killed, which amounts to 3,700 assassinated. The program was created by the CIA, but was carried-out by a special secret police force operated by the South Vietnamese government and military, keeping the US involvement at a minimum. The police force was used to interrogate and torture suspected Viet Cong to get information. Meanwhile, the CIA Director Richard Helms and William Colby assured the President that the Phoenix Program did not torture suspects, but only detained or de-programed suspected VC. They also said they only assassinated key high ranking officials, (14%) in order for the program to work as intended, which was to cause chaos within the Viet Cong infrastructure.

The South Vietnamese military and political groups used the Phoenix Program for personal purposes, such as neutralizing political opposition or people they deemed anti-government. There was criticism concerning that random village leaders were systematically killed if they suspected them of harboring VC. The overall goal and purpose was to meet the 1,800 monthly quotas. It was also rumored that entire villages were purged if they found stockpiles of weapons and ammunition in the village which placed the entire village in group C. It had long since been rumored that My Lai and My Khe and My Son may have been among the villages targeted in the Phoenix program as I will point out later.

The CIA Phoenix coordinator and operative in the region was a man named Ramsdell. According to the Peers Investigation Panel investigating the My Lai Massacre; Ramsdell told Intelligence Officer, Captain Kotouc, who in return told Lt. Colonel Frank Barker that "Only VC and active VC sympathizers were living in My Lai and My Khe." Ramsdell supplied the information to company headquarters for implementation (cleansing). He also went on to say that they dropped leaflets instructing civilians and non VC out of the villages by 0700 hours, and anyone who remained after 0700 hours would be considered VC. [73] **[Footnote 9]**

Ramsdell also told the Peers Panel, "Frankly, anyone that was in that area was considered a Viet Cong Suspect, because they couldn't survive in that area unless they were sympathizers." Ramsdell provided Captain Kotouc a blacklist of Viet Cong Suspects in My Lai and My Khe and that the Viet Cong sympathizers would be gone by 0700 hours on the morning of March 16th and only the 450 hard-core VC guerillas would remain behind". This was contrary to the VC mode of operation of hit and run. [73]

During the peak of Operation Phoenix, there were 4,000 recruited into the program and were commanded by US Military officers and senior NCO's. After 1969, the command was turned-over to CIA advisers, which indicates that there was a break-down in the program and leaks in the operation.

One segment of the program built Provincial Interrogation Centers (PIC), in each of the Provinces. Another segment of the program was called Hamlet Informant Project (HIP).

The purpose of this program was to recruit spies in each of the villages to inform on any of the residents if they were Viet Cong or Viet Cong sympathizers. If the suspect was interrogated and found not to be a VC, then the informant would not get paid a bounty. The informant only got paid if the suspect admitted he was a VC. [19]

There were literally dozens of covert operations going on simultaneously in Vietnam while the Phoenix Program was in operation. Some were the "brain child" of the CIA and others were Special Forces and military operations that were classified as secret. Very few were marginally successful and made little difference in the outcome of the war. When the Phoenix Program began, it was to incorporate the dozen programs into one large one. But there were so many spy agencies involved in Vietnam that it never materialized as expected, and the results were questionable at best.

The CIA touted that the Phoenix Program was a big success, but in reality it had marginal success. Near the end of the War, more and more NVA moved into South Vietnam to replace the VC who had been assassinated under the Phoenix program, realizing that America's role in Vietnam would soon be over. As pressure built toward eradication of the VC, by 1969 and 1970, most fled across the border into Cambodia and established camps and ammo dumps out of reach of American forces.

At that stage in the war, there was little need for a guerrilla war and the use of VC guerrillas. By 1969, only a handful of VC remained in the tunnels. North Vietnam was in firm control of 45% of the country and was planning an all-out take-over as soon as the American's pulled out. In keeping with Nixon's campaign policy of ending the Vietnam War, North Vietnam just had to wait a few more years, and the prize would be theirs.

Operation Eldest Son

One rogue project called "Eldest Son" and "Pole Green and Italian Green" which was partially successful, but more entertaining than anything. The Studies and Observation Group, SOG had come up with a plan under the direction of Colonel Singlaub who had a laboratory on Kadena Air Force Base in Okinawa. [20]

The program involved sabotaging captured ammunition stockpiles for use by the NVA and VC along the Ho Chi Minh Trail. They would remove existing powder from the shells and replace it with a much more powerful powder which would explode in the firearm in the hands of the unsuspecting user, was often fatal. During the course of the program, 11,500 AK-47 cartridges, 550 machine gun cartridges and 2,000 mortar shells were sabotaged.

To avoid detection, they would randomly place several bad cartridges in each case, so they would not know which cartridge was bad. Since not knowing for sure which were good and bad, they were forced to abandon the entire stockpile. As it turned out through captured communications between North Vietnam and Beijing, the ammunition was originally manufactured in China, so Ho Chi Minh accused China of manufacturing substandard ammunition. They cancelled all of China's Ammo orders and purchased their Ammunition from Russia. It is not known for certain how many were killed as a result of the sabotaged ammo, but it did cause considerable chaos and finger pointing in the leadership in North Vietnam headquarters.

The Tunnels

The Vinh Moc and Cu Chi tunnels became a tourist attraction after the war, but during the Vietnam War it was a strategic network of underground tunnels of limestone silt that allowed the Viet Cong guerrillas to go underground to hide from patrols and B-52 bombing raids.

Contrary to popular folk lore being told tourist today, the VC and the tunnels had little overall impact on the war itself as related to the US military operation especially after the TET offensive of 1968. Shortly after the TET offensive in the winter of 1968, Operation Phoenix decimated much of the operational effectiveness of the VC and the tunnel network. The tunnels would later be used by the NVA as the number of VC declined with the loss of 68,000 VC in 1968 alone. Many VC moved into Saigon and carried out bombing raids on government buildings and assassinations and kidnappings of government officials. However the mystiques of the tunnels remain, and it has become one of the most popular tourist attractions in Vietnam today. There were two major tunnel systems in Vietnam; the Vinh Moc tunnels in the Quang Tri Valley in central Vietnam and the Cu Chi tunnels, 30 miles south of Ho Chi Minh City (Saigon). Each tunnel system covered as much as 75 miles of tunnel network in multiple levels that contained water wells, kitchens, medical clinics, planning rooms and rooms for sleeping. In the Vinh Moc Tunnels, it was capable of housing 60 families (300 people) who lived below ground.

The tunnels were also used as a military staging area for above ground operations, where maps of military bases, hit lists, troop movements and locations of American and allied troops movements were kept. A small store of weapons was kept in the tunnels. The tunnels were too small to store large stockpiles of military supplies, but were used primarily for guerrilla warfare operations for "hit and run" operations.

The tunnels were heavily fortified with "booby traps" for unsuspecting "tunnel rats" who would go below and seek out the enemy hiding in the tunnels. South Vietnamese soldiers were most often used because of their size, since most Americans and allied troops were too large to fit into the tunnels, and once entering the tunnels it was impossible to back-out, unless you knew the lay-out of the tunnel system. Life in the tunnels was a miserable existence. A captured document stated that half of those living in the tunnels suffered from malaria in which all had intestinal parasites of a severe nature. Some even suffered blindness after the war as a result of being in the dark for long periods o   such as "black lung" from the dust and oil burning lamps used in confined spaces. But the tunnels did create havoc while they were in existence, but much of the f time. Some even developed lung problems, distress caused during the war was due by villagers who provide a safe harbor for the VC, which was too difficult to discern who the enemy was. As a result of political disorganization, it would play into the hands of the North Vietnamese and their recruitment efforts in the South. [77]

Paris Peace Agreement

When Richard Nixon became President, he used the bombing of North Vietnam as a tool to force North and South Vietnam to sit down and negotiate a peace settlement. The first peace negotiations took place in 1968, which may have been a stall tactic pioneered by both Mao Zedong and Chiang Kai-shek in the 1930's and 40's to halt or slow-down the invasion of the Japanese in the Second Sino-Japanese War of 1937.

Victory celebration, as the NVA marched down the streets of Saigon on April 30, 1975. Fig 9C

Mao Zedong, sent advisers to North Vietnam as early as 1950 to train NVA (North Vietnam Army) and Viet Congo (VC) how to fight guerrilla warfare. Mao wrote and published a book, "How to fight Guerrilla Warfare" which sold for 10 cents a copy in China (available today on Amazon.com). One of Mao's lessons was how to stall peace negotiations while building up and strengthening military positions to take advantage of a cease fire agreement. Mao believed that negotiating peace agreements were made to be broken for the purpose of a military advantage in building troops strength. This tactic was used by North Vietnam with great skill and treachery as outlined in Mao's book. A good example was when the Paris Peace talks adjourned in 1968, North Vietnam insisted that a round table rather than a rectangular table be used during the peace negotiations. Peace talks stalled until a compromised was reached, where a round table with rectangular side tables placed behind each member was a finally agreed to before peace could begin. They also demanded that all bombing cease while the negotiations were taking place. It was a strategic plan to stall negotiations while the NVA was moving men and supplies south without interference from bombing their supply route.

On January 27, 1973 the Paris Peace Agreement was signed after 5 years of negotiations. But in the shadows of the negotiations, President Nixon secretly offered Vietnam $3.3 billion dollars in War reparations to North Vietnam. Former US Presidents rejected the War reparations, claiming that Vietnam's invasion of Cambodia and the Violation of the Paris Peace Agreement by invading South Vietnam voided the payment. In addition, Vietnams failure to return the war dead and prisoners of war violated the Geneva Convention. At the time of the signing of the Paris Peace Agreement in January of 1973, the South Vietnamese Armed Forces had 920,000 active troops and North Vietnam left 219,000 VC and NVA in South Vietnam.

Forty years has passed since the Paris Peace Agreement was signed, President Nixon's edited transcripts of his White House Tape Conversations; revealed that in 1968, while running as a presidential candidate, he ordered Anna Chennault, the liaison to the South Vietnam government to persuade President Thieu to reject a cease-fire agreement between President Johnson and North Vietnam, which may have led to a permanent peace agreement. In 1797, President John Adams sponsored a bill in congress called the Logan Act. The purpose of the Act was to keep private citizens from intruding in official government negotiations with a foreign nation. A person or persons violating the Act would be charged with treason which could be subject to death.

Nixon's sabotage of the peace talks was confirmed by transcripts of FBI wire taps, which in essence said; "not to negotiate, I will give you a better deal when I am elected." On November 2, 1968, LBJ received the report from the FBI. On November 3, Johnson confronted Nixon, and he denied the accusations. [81]

President Johnson wanted to prosecute Nixon on charges of treason, but was talked out of doing do so by Secretary of Defense, Clark Clifford who felt that the riots over the Vietnam War and a former Vice President running for President being charged for treason could cause serious political consequences. It would become buried and kept secret for 40 years.

After Nixon was elected, he established the "plumbers unit" whose purpose was to stop leaks in the White House, that could have political consequences. The plumbers' would later be caught breaking into the Democratic National Committee at Watergate in 1972, which would force President Nixon's resignation in 1974 over the Watergate scandal.

Vietnam's Re-education Camps

Even though Saigon fell to the North Vietnamese communist on April 30, 1975, the Vietnamese communist wasted little time in establishing and building more than 300 re-education camps through-out South Vietnam to help assimilate former South Vietnamese into the new communist society. These camps were in fact work camps and prisoner of war camps. While it was believed that many would be brain-washed and accept the new society for which most were completely unfamiliar, there would be those that would need to be purged. Vietnam kept these camps secret from the outside world and would only allow reporters from Russia and China to visit them. As was characteristic with communist countries, the reporters were only shown a model camp where inmates would be laying around playing soccer, cards, watching movies and reading communist literature, when in fact they weren't prisoners at all, but North Vietnamese soldiers dressed in prison uniforms. The camps were nothing more than extermination camps and designed to revenge former South Vietnamese military officers, soldiers and political prisoners who fought side by side with America.

Prisoners were required to sign confessions and be interviewed periodically to see if their attitude had changed toward communism and against America. On the average most detainees remained in the camps between three to four years, however if they failed there interviews, they would remain another four years or longer until eventual death if necessary. Torture was part of the re-education program, as well as starvation. More than 500,000 prisoners had extended stays in the camps and more than 65,000 were executed from 1975 to 1983 according to the US State Department. One Berkeley researcher reported that the camps were "a sophisticated form of "drip death" that the communist regimes used for liquidating class enemies." [76]

One prisoner said that in his camp, there were 300 military colonels and two and a half years later there were only 37 remained. In the early 1980's the United States negotiated with Vietnam to have thousands of prisoners deported from Vietnam's re-education camps to the United States, only then was the full extent of life in the camps revealed.

One prisoner said. "At least Pol Pot kills people quickly, whereas the Vietnamese preferred to kill you slowly over time." This was a reoccurring theme that many of the survivors echoed when they arrived in America and were debriefed by State Department Officials.

The war in Vietnam is now history and most of the Vietnamese living today weren't born when the War was being played out. Only a few war Museums and tunnels and battle sites remain, but few remember the thousands who lost their lives for a cause yet to be fully understood. What we have learned from all this is that time heals and sometimes our former enemies become our friends, even when their ideology and culture is paradoxical.

The Vietnam War Moves to America

After the fall of Saigon in 1975, the United States accepted 125,000 high ranking South Vietnamese military and civilian personnel and families to immigrate to the United States. Most were sent to Texas and California, with the remainder scattered from Florida to Seattle. A second and third wave of Vietnamese immigrants arrived later, but most were Vietnamese boat people fleeing the communist regime, who were unskilled and had family contacts in the America.

The Vietnamese assimilated into American society better than most other immigrants. However, like other immigrant groups, they established their own communities of stores and newspapers and social groups and clubs. Unlike other ethnic immigrants, the Vietnamese were displaced as a result of a communist take-over of their country, so they had a deep resentment toward communism, and in particular the North Vietnamese and Chinese. A network of former South Vietnamese military leaders continued to advocate the overthrow of the North Vietnamese government and would hold regular meetings on how to accomplish it. The US Government didn't discourage their enthusiasm, partly because they already had "freedom fighters" on the ground in Cambodia being led by a man named Pol Pot and his Khmer Rouge, who was fighting a guerrilla war against the Vietnamese who invaded Cambodia in 1978. The Khmer Rouge under Pol Pot did little or nothing to re-take Cambodia from

Vietnam other than collecting US military aid and terrorize local Cambodian villages along the border of Thailand.

The American Vietnamese created their own organization called the "Vietnamese Organization to Exterminate Communist and Restore the Nation" (VOECRN). The America Vietnamese (VOECRN) claimed they had a guerrilla camp in Laos and in Vietnam where they were covertly fighting Vietnamese communist. They actively solicited money from American Vietnamese businesses and Vietnamese immigrants to keep the covert war going for years. In the end, most of the fighters were killed and the millions of dollars collected evaporated along with their hopes of a democratic Vietnam.

From July of 1981 to September of 1990, 5 American Vietnamese were assassinated in the United States. Two were killed in California, one in Texas and two in Virginia. There were a total of 5 murders and 7 attempted murders. The FBI classified VOECRN as a terrorist organization; however, it appears that the FBI may have turned a blind eye toward VOECRN's activities in the US. When a newspaper requested a Freedom of Information request from the FBI concerning their investigations into VOECRN, they refused on the grounds of national security. This may explain why the murder cases were never solved. I suspect the FBI or CIA may have had a clandestine operation going on at the time which involved members of the VOECRN.

Douglas G Beaudoin

Chapter 8

Laos: The Secret War

The Lao people began to migrate from Southeast China around the 8th century. They were of the Thai Kadai ancestry from Southeast China. In the 14th century the first Laotian state was founded. By 1713 the country was split into three separate states. It fell under Thai rule in the 18th century and became a French protectorate in 1893. After World War II, it became a constitutional Monarchy.

In 1951, Prince Souphanouvong organized a Communist independence movement called the Pathet Lao in North Vietnam. Once organized, the Viet Minh and the Pathet Lao communist invaded northeastern Laos that fueled a civil war between the Pathet Lao and the nationalist under Prince Souvanna Phouma, the Royal Prime Minister. By 1960, it became a three-way war between the Pathet Lao communist, Pro-western revolutionary government headed by Prince Boun Qum and the Laos Royal Government under General Nosavan.

The secret war ended up not being secret after all. It involved the Royal Laos Government, backed by the CIA against the Communist Pathet Lao. In June of 1962, Laos and Cambodia declared its neutrality at the Geneva Conference. The CIA's Air America Airlines was in Laos under the cloak of being a humanitarian Aid operation (USAID) that provided food, cargo and transportation to the indigenous people of the mountains, known as the Hmong (mong) and other hill tribe people. In fact, it did provide food aid to the indigenous tribes, along with military support along with military weapons and supplies.

When the French vacated Indochina in 1954, the Royal Lao Government was recognized as the ruling government of Laos by the Geneva Convention of 1954. As a result of the Convention, Vietnam was divided into North and South Vietnam along the 17th Parallel. Prince Souvanna Phouma was a neutralist and was appointed Prime Minister of Laos after French pulled out of Indochina. The US State Department was afraid that a small communist group would gain a foot hold in the government and eventually take over because of a rebel communist group known as the Pathet Lao. When elections were held in 1956, the Pathet Lao were excluded from elections and Prince Souvanna easily won the reelection. With the growing tension and the steady infiltration of the North Vietnamese in the east to assist the Pathet Lao, Prince Souvanna realized that he needed to fix the problem else the Communist will take over the government by force. He decided to hold a series of supplementary elections that would integrate the Pathet Lao into the Royal Army and into key positions in government. It was all done to pacify the communist faction and avoid further infiltration of the North Vietnamese by North Vietnam.

For the next few years, Prince Souvanna was seen in Hanoi and Beijing, even though declaring Laos a neutral state. The US Government was financing the entire Laos Royal Military to fight the Communist and became upset as a result. Kennedy threatened to cut off foreign aid and military aid when Prince Souvanna became friendly with China and North Vietnam. The US government decided to take a more active role in the politics of Laos by organizing a covert operation in Laos that would stop the flow of the North Vietnam military.

Kennedy's War in Laos

In 1959, the Kennedy sent a special force of 107 men into Laos wearing civilian clothes to train the Laos Royal Military in unconventional warfare against the Pathet Lao. This was at the request of the Laos government, and it was revealed that the Pathet Lao were dug-in near the Plain of Jars in the East near the Vietnam border. A guerrilla war broke-out with "hit and run" tactics used by Viet Cong (VC) in South Vietnam in 1960. President Kennedy authorized the deployment of 16,000 military advisors into Vietnam to train the South Vietnamese Army to help South Vietnam build an effective fighting force to counter the North Vietnamese insurgency. The Geneva Convention of 1954 limited foreign military intervention into Laos, Cambodia because of their declared neutrality. Kennedy was committed to honor the Geneva agreements; however he was explicit in expressing to the America people that stopping communist aggression in Southeast Asia was his highest priority.

Many claim that had Kennedy been alive, he would not have allowed ground troops into Vietnam as his predecessor, LBJ had. However it is pure speculation, but, it is reasonable to assume he would have taken a more aggressive role in the training and developing the South Vietnamese Army into a much more effective fighting force called Vietnamization. Kennedy wanted to begin Vietnamization as early as 1963. Kennedy was distressed in learning the fate of President Diem's assassination in South Vietnam in 1963, and even though he knew of his corruption and poor public relation skills that destroyed the morale and spirit of the South Vietnamese Army, was able to bring stability and leadership.

President Kennedy authorized the CIA to conduct a highly secret and classified war in Laos under the auspices of being a humanitarian relief organization, called "USAID". The secret CIA air force was called Air America and Continental Air Services and was headquartered in Udon Thani, Thailand, which was only 35 miles from Laos's border and its capital, Vientiane. The head of command was under William H. Sullivan who was the Ambassador to Laos and stationed in Vientiane. The secret city, called Long Tien, was constructed deep into the jungle of Laos in which CIA field agents and Air America pilots would stage missions using old T-28, C-123 and short-takeoff and landing aircraft to ferry food, medical supplies and military equipment to ground troops. To fight the insurgents, General Vang Pao was recruited to take charge of the ground troops who were mainly Meo (Mong) tribesmen. He had fought alongside the French in Vietnam and was invaluable in recruiting soldiers from an ethnic hill tribe villages for which Vang Pao was one himself. The Meo were loyal anti-communist guerrilla fighters, made famous during the French-Vietnam War of the early 50's and were known to have unshakable courage under fire.

Souvanna Phouma, who was very popular and among the people easily won re-election in 1956. It was noticed by American military advisors that the Royal Laos Army would go for days or weeks without conducting sorties or going on patrols to confront insurgents. In one situation, the North Vietnamese insurgents set-up a camp only miles from the Royal Laos Military Base in central Laos. It soon became apparent that the Laos government was using the United States as a means of financial support for their Royal Lao Military and would only provide token military resistance in order to keep the money rolling-in from the U.S.. In 1959, U.S. Special Forces found that the communist insurgents were "dug-in" 100 miles from the Capital of Vientiane, in an area called the Plain of Jars.

In 1960, elections were held and Poumi was elected Prime Minister. Criticism surfaced that the CIA was involved in vote rigging and the situation was resolved when a Army Captain in the Royal Laos Army named Kong Le, orchestrate a Coup d'état and remove Poumi and re-install Prince Souvanna as Prime Minister. The U.S. realized that the Royal Laos Military would only fight a half-hearted war. The CIA and President Kennedy was briefed by former President Eisenhower, who said that Laos was a key element in stopping the spread of communism through-out Asia. Failure to do so would lead to all of Southeast Asia becoming communist. What few realized at the time, Eisenhower took his hat off as President and became General Eisenhower when he gave advise to Kennedy when he left office. Eisenhower's skill in the military was not that of a fighting General as Patton, but rather a logistics General. He must have known that the communist needed Laos in order to use it as a supply route in providing troops, supplies and military equipment into South Vietnam and Cambodia if they were to win the war against the Americans.

General Vang Pao recruited about 30,000 to 40,000 Meo soldiers from the rural villages throughout Laos to fight the communist insurgents. The Pathet Laos communist only had about 15,000 volunteers who were yet un-trained and inexperienced and couldn't possibly match the Meo guerrilla fighters. As the guerrilla war continued, the North Vietnamese entered the war by infiltrating thousands of North Vietnam (NVA) soldiers into Northeastern Laos to assist the Pathet Lao.

In the interim, the United States sent 666 military advisers into Laos in 1961. By 1962, more than 6,000 North Vietnamese soldiers were fighting alongside the Pathet Lao. In 1962, Prime Minister, Souvanna Phouma and delegates from China, North Vietnam, Soviet Union and the United States, convened in Geneva and signed the Geneva Accord of 1962, which re-instated Laos neutrality, in which all foreign nations who had military personnel in Laos were to leave. The United States moved 666 military advisors out of Laos, while North Vietnam moved only 6 North Vietnamese troops out of Laos.

It became clear to the United States that Prime Minister Souvanna Phouma had aligned himself toward communism, using the Geneva Conference to expel American forces and allowing North Vietnam to remain without contesting their presence. North Vietnam insisted that they had no troops in Laos and that there was no such thing as the Ho Chi Minh Trail, both of which was a flagrant lie and the U.S. knew it, but didn't press the issue.

Even though it was apparent that the North Vietnamese had not moved their troops out of Laos, the United States could have moved in ground troops without the consent of Laos's Prime Minister, Souvanna Phouma. The Hague Convention of 1907 establishes rules of war that allows a foreign country to invade should another foreign country occupy a country who declared itself as a neutral country. Kennedy failed to enact the rules of war under the Hague Convention of 1907, but rather decided to use a covert operation to fight communist insurgents.

The importance of forcing the North Vietnam out of Laos would have a devastating effect in the war in Vietnam. Had the U.S. forcibly moved the North Vietnamese troops out of Laos and controlled the border between North Vietnam and Laos, the North Vietnamese would be unable to construct the Ho Chi Minh Trail which would have been their only supply route for military troops and supplies and equipment into South Vietnam. Ho Chi Minh stated that they would lose the war had they not had the Trail. Eisenhower made it clear to Kennedy when leaving office that it is imperative that the key to Southeast Asia was keeping Laos out of the hands of the communist. Laos bordered North Vietnam, South Vietnam, Cambodia, China, Burma and Thailand. It was the transportation corridor to Southeast Asia for insurgents.

I assume Kennedy did not want to accelerate the war in Laos, especially when Vietnam was also under the threat of a communist insurgency. His actions illustrates that he would much rather use CIA covert operations over deployment of US ground troops in both Laos and Vietnam. Both Laos and South Vietnam were having frequent turn-over in leadership and governments which made it difficult to get political support from the government who preferred US military rather than ground troops to fight the insurgents. Much of the aid money was squandered and was not directed toward improving their own military defense.

Air America, CIA's private Air force

Civil Air Transport (CAT) began air operations in 1950 in China after World War II. It was funded by the CIA during the Korean War. CAT was started by General Claire Chennault who was the commanding General of the 14th U.S. Air Corp during World War II. He was the former leader of the "Flying Tigers" during the early part of World War II, flying missions from Burma into China after Japan invaded China in 1937. CAT changed its name to Air America in 1959, as part of the covert operation by the CIA and moved its headquarters to Udon Thani Air Force Base in Thailand, where the CIA had offices. They also set up Satellite office in Vientiane where the US Ambassador to Laos had his office. There was a field operations airport in Long Tien, Laos.

During its peak of operations, Long Tien Airport was among the busiest airports in the world, yet it never appeared on any map. Air America's real role was to provide cargo and military supplies to the Hill Tribe Hmong people who were fighting the communist insurgents infiltrating from North Vietnam. Even though its real mission was combat support, the rest of the world was told it was providing humanitarian Aid to the displaced Hill Tribe people of Laos, which for the most part was true. Over a period of several years, the airline accumulated 24 cargo airplanes and 24 short takeoff and landing aircraft (STOL) for use in remote airports and 30 helicopters and 300 pilots and hundreds of support personnel.

The hill tribe people of Laos made most of their living growing poppies for opium. Prior to the Vietnam War, most of the opium was used for personal consumption, but during the Vietnam War, Air America provided the transportation logistics to Bangkok and Saigon where the heroine ended up in the hands of American troops in South Vietnam in which the drug lords were South Vietnam government officials.

Opium was light weight when processed, and was easily be carried off the mountains and into the city from a small bush airport, where a broker or agent would pay cash to the villager at the airport before loading it on the plane for further distribution. The broker or agent would purchase raw opium and send it to lab in Vientiane or the golden triangle, to be processed into heroin. The heroin moved from the golden Triangle into Thailand to a major airport like Bangkok or Saigon for worldwide distribution.

Air America built small dirt bush air strips in dozens of small Hmong villages so they could deliver humanitarian aid as well as a few dozen cases of arms and hand grenades. This was a perfect operation for the back-haul of opium. The villagers needed someone they trusted to take the opium from the planes when it arrived at the Air America base. They needed someone with unlimited access to the base and who could come and go freely without any questions being ask. This person was said to be General Vang Pao.

To fight the Communist Pathet Laos, the CIA needed a Charismatic Laos military leader to take charge of the military operation on behalf of the Nationalist Laos. It was to be a guerilla run operation of hit and run, since the insurgents had a much larger and potentially expanding military force, fed by North Vietnam. General Vang Pao was a Hmong military leader who was a commander in the French Infantry Battalion in Laos in the 1950's. He was a World War II veteran who fought a guerilla war against the Japanese during World War II as well.

Vang Pao was popular among the indigenous Meo hill tribe people, since he was a Hmong (pronounced mong) himself. While the CIA was paying General Vang Pao and the Hmong fighters to fight the insurgents, it was rumored that he also had a side business as a cash crop broker for the Hmong and hill tribe people in the Opium trade. This fact today is still hotly debated by CIA, however, eye witness accounts by pilots and CIA agents, such as Tony Poe and Ron Rickenbach of the US Aid and Development Program, also known as USAID say otherwise.

CIA turned a blind-eye to Vang Pao's activities because he was much too valuable to the US Government as a military General and recruiter in the fight against the Pathet Lao. A few indiscretions could be overlooked and many were. This wasn't the first time that the CIA was accused of being involved in transporting drugs, at least perhaps not knowingly.

The company, Sea Supply and Civil Air Transport (CAT for short) was established by Paul Helliwell and was based in Taiwan. It was owned by the CIA for the purpose of providing military supplies and raising money for Chiang Kai-shek's army in Taiwan. Since it was difficult to raise enough money by providing sea and air cargo services, Helliwell said the money could be made by transporting drugs to Chiang Kai-Shek. It has been said that they would fly arms into Burma and back haul heroin into Bangkok, Saigon and Taiwan for Chiang Kai-shek, who financed the war against the Communist on the mainland of China in the early 1950's. It may have continued even after fleeing to Taiwan.

The CIA's, Air America Airlines built up its fleet overtime, but after the Geneva Accord of 1962, Laos reaffirmed their neutrality and the United States was forced to pull back all of their military advisors and close down the military facilities and airports in Laos. This meant that Air America had to lay off pilots and aircrews and sell some of its planes. The US allowed only two military observers to remain in Laos to insure that the terms of the Geneva agreement were being complied with.

In 1963, reports were coming in from the Hmong and by aerial reconnaissance that more than 7,000 North Vietnamese regulars had moved in the area known as the Plain of Jars, in eastern Laos, near the Laos and Vietnam borders. This was a clear violation of the 1962 Geneva neutrality agreement. The US once again began to activate their secret air force, Air America. Congress authorized additional funding to Air America of one hundred forty six million dollars per year.

The secret war in Laos was actually was two separate wars. One war was trying to stop the North Vietnamese from bring supplies south along the Ho Chi Minh Trail and the other was between the Royal Lao Army battling the Pathet Lao communist for control of the Laos and the Laos government.

General Vang Pao had gone to all of the villages and recruited Hmong and other indigenous hill tribe people to fight against the communist. Air America's role was to provide air transport service for military cargo, and supplies to the Hmong and hill tribe villages. In doing so, Vang Pao gave them a monthly salary and rice to feed their families while they were away fighting. In addition, they would help broker their cash crop (opium) and take it to market. As the war continued, the casualty rate had increased from 40,000 to as little as 4,000. Vang Pao returned to the villages and recruited more Hmong, but all that was left were 14 year old boys. He told the villages to give- up the boys else he would cut off their rice and food stipends.

The villagers were angry but had little recourse but to give Vang Pao the young boys for duty into Vang Pao's army. As more and more rumors were being circulated about Vang Pao and the Royal Lao Army Commanders, General Quane Rattikone became involved in the heroin business, and the US Government became uncomfortable in their close association and wanted to distance them as much as possible. They organized a meeting in which Vang Pao and the CIA agreed to give him his own Airline Company.

The CIA was concerned that if an Air America plane crashed it would fall into the wrong hands and create an awkward situation in explaining how drugs got on board. To keep Vang Pao and General Rattikone happy, the CIA delivered a freshly painted C-47 with a new Airline name; "Zieng Khouang Air Transport Company". It would later be known as "Opium Air". Vang Pao's joint ventured with General Quan Rattikone was very profitable and they acquired more C-47 aircraft over time.

A typical Hill Tribe Village, on the Burma and Thai border   Fig. 10

By 1973, they had six Douglas C-47's. The drug trade in Laos was eventually traced to South Vietnam and President Nguyen Van Thieu. By 1970, more than 33% of the American troops in South Vietnam would become addicted to heroin, which was traced back to the Golden Triangle in Laos, and most certainly Vang Pao and his well-connected associates.

The Golden Triangle

The name Golden Triangle is area where the borders of Myanmar (Burma), Thailand and Laos meet, which forms triangle between the Mekong River and the Kok River. In reality it covers an area about the size of Oregon (98,000 sq. miles) more or less.

It is a mountainous terrain and ideal for cultivating poppies, which is the origin of opium and a refined version called heroin. The opium poppy is native to Southeast Asia but some believe it was introduced by Dutch traders in the 1700's. Most of the opium cultivation was done by the hill tribe people of Southeast Asia, in particular the Shan and Hmong hill tribe people.

Britain was active in the Teak lumber trade in Burma and Thailand in the late 1700 and 1800's and soon became the main trader and exporter of opium into China for their opium dens.

It was British traders who introduced opium to China as well as tobacco and pipes that were used to inhale the opium. Opium dens became common place throughout China and Southeast Asia by the end of the 19th century. The main reason British traders used opium was because it was easy to sell opium to the Chinese for cash rather than trading product for product. The British merchants on the other hand paid the Chinese cash for products such as tea, spices and fabric but only wanted to trade for products made in Britain.

Mekong River, Golden Triangle, Thailand in the foreground, Laos on the right and Myanmar (Burma) on the left   Fig. 11

What British traders needed cash to purchase products from the Chinese, and opium was the product that helped the trade balance. That may be where the original term "cash crop" came from. Even though China eventually banned opium and opium imports, the British traders smuggled it into China and demanded an even higher price for it. After the Chinese and British Opium Wars of 1840's and 1860's, it was once again legalized in China, so it was business as usual for British traders.

. The King of the Triangle

The king of the Golden Triangle was Khun Sa. He was of Shan Burmese and Chinese ancestry and lived in Northern Myanmar and became infamous as one of the most notorious drug and war lords in Asia.

When Mao Zedong took control of China in 1948, many nationalist under the command of Chiang Kai-shek and the Kuomintang (KMT) party fled to Taiwan and the border countries of Laos, Thailand and Burma (Myanmar) with the hopes of mounting a counter attack against the communist. In 1960, Khun Sa joined the Kuomintang (KMT) and lived in the Shan State in Northern Burma.

The Kuomintang had no money to support themselves and their political cause, so they resorted to opium as their primary source of income. In 1963, Khun Sa formed his own army know as Ka Kwe Ye Militia, which was financed by General Ne Win's Burmese Government, however as his army became larger, he decided not support the government and instead focus on a more profitable trade, such as drugs. In 1969 he was captured by the government and was released in 1973 after his men had captured two Russian doctors and held them captive in exchange for Khun Sa's release. In 1976, he moved his drug operation to the village of Ban Hin Taek on the Thai border. By 1985 he was the largest drug lord in the Golden Triangle. For years he produced and sold drugs internationally until he got the attention of DEA in the United States.

In October of 1982, 39 Thai Rangers with the support of the U.S. Drug Enforcement Administration (DEA), attempted to assassinate Khun Sa, but the attempt failed and Khun Sa moved his drug operation back across the border into Myanmar where he would be safe from DEA and the Thai Army. There were about 6 or 7 labs in operation around the Golden Triangle where opium was refined into heroin, most of which was part of Khun Sa's operation. Most of the heroin would be transported to Bangkok, Rangoon or Saigon and distributed worldwide. [50]

In 1989, Khun Sa was charged and indicted in New York Federal Court in absentia for importing 1,000 tons of heroin into the USA. It was determined that 80% of the heroin entering the US was from Khun Sa's drug operation. Myanmar, however, would not honor the extradition of Khun Sa to the United States. He was well protected by the Myanmar Government and there was little doubt that Khun Sa was paying government officials for his protections.

From 1974 to 1996, Khun Sa recruited a rebel force of 18,000 troops and a local militia of 8,000. His drug empire was one of the largest in the world. Khun Sa died in October of 2007 in Yangon at 73. I was reported that he had diabetes and other chronic ailments which attributed to his death. Khun Sa had eight children to carry on his drug empire. His legacy of drug smuggling continues today and out of the reach of the Burmese Military in which his drug empire pays handsomely for their anonymity.

The Legend of Tony Poe

In 1979, the movie "Apocalypse Now", directed by Francis Ford Coppola and starring Marlon Brando as Colonel Kurts and Charles Sheen as Captain Willard became an instant box office success. A lot of speculation was circulated after the Vietnam War and a CIA operative named Anthony Poshepny alias Anthony Alexander alias Tony Poe whom the character sounded very similar to Colonel Kurts in the movie. Coppola maintains that the Colonel Kurts character loosely followed a Special Forces Colonel in Vietnam whose name was Robert Rheault. He became known in the media in 1969 after being arrested for the murder of a suspected double agent in Vietnam.

However, many believe that Colonel Kurts alias Tony Poe was the real Colonel Kurts. Poe as he was later called, arrived in Laos in 1961 after spending time in Indonesia for the CIA. He was known in CIA circles as agent Upin or Pat Gibbs. His job in Laos was to organize and provide logistics behind a desk, and to stay out of combat. Poe was never one to follow orders and performed best on his own away from supervision. He was a World War II veteran and was shot in the battle of Iwo Jima. He also served during the Korean War as a CIA operative and now was given an assignment in Laos. He operated out of a base camp deep into jungles of northern Laos near the Chinese border.

Rumors were circulating back at headquarters in Udon Thani, Thailand about Poe's unorthodox and macabre methods he used on the enemy during combat. He paid his men one dollar for an enemy's ear. He weaved the ears on a string and stretched them along the eve of the porch roof like Christmas Lights. One day while on patrol, he happened upon a ten year old Hmong boy and noticed he had no ears. Poe asked the boy what happened to his ears, and the boy replied that his father needed money and heard they were paying money for ears and he chopped them off. Poe said from that day on he stopped paying for ears. However, he decided to raise the price to 10 dollars for enemy heads wearing a Pathet Lao caps. When his superiors in Vientiane confronted him about his unorthodox methods to motivate troops, he sent an envelope filled with ears and a note that read, "here is your proof that we are really out here doing our job," of course, it was a hot day and when the mail arrived at headquarters on a Friday afternoon, everyone had gone home for the weekend, which allowed the ears to ferment in the hot sun in the box.   Two days later, on a Monday morning, the secretary arrived and opened the envelope and began vomiting.

As a training exercise for his guerrillas, he placed an enemy head on a pole so that his troops could throw rocks at it.   When confronted about this training methods and technique, he said it was a method of reinforcing the troop's anti-communist fervor.   On two separate occasions, he flew over the enemy and dropped severed enemy heads out of the door of the aircraft on to the porch of the enemy.   His reasoning was to instill fear for the Hmong hill tribe people, so they would think twice before they would invade their villages.   Surprisingly, in most cases it worked, or at least while Tony Poe was in charge.

He had been shot 3 times and survived, and had his fingers blown off trying to disarm a booby trap, he claims it was meant for him. He claimed Americans were trying to assassinate him, however it was perhaps not true, but added to the mystique of the Tony Poe legend. In reality he lost his fingers demonstrating to the Hmong troops how to defuse a booby trap.   Before his death in 2003, he maintained that the CIA believed he had gone rogue and that the booby trap was meant for him.   He claimed that the government had sent Special Forces to kill him on 3 different occasions, but failed.   There is no proof of these allegations, but it did fuel the speculation that he was the real Colonel Kurts and bigger than life.   The hill tribe people of Northern Laos today, believe Tony Poe lives and he cannot be killed.

Poe married a Hmong Princess from one of the villages, which was in defiance of CIA policy. His superiors tried to recall him back to the main office in Vientiane, Laos but to no avail. Poe stayed in Laos until March of 1973, at which time his base camp became overrun by Pathet Lao. A day later he had his base camp bombed with Napalm. He moved to Thailand and lived there with his wife for 15 years, after which, he returned to the US with his wife, where he died in 2003 at the age of 80 in Sonoma, California.

After the communist took over Laos the Hmong hill tribe people were hunted down relentlessly by the Laos Government. More than 10,000 Hmong were executed for their role in the secret war by the Lao government.

Most Hmong crossed into Thailand for protection against reprisal by the communist government of Laos. Even today, a small army of Hmong still hold-out in the jungles of northern Laos, and are still fighting the communist. A journalist went into the jungle to film documentary about the secret war, and ran across hundreds of Hmong fighters in a village who thought the reporter was Tony Poe and fell on their knees crying as if he were god. Tony Poe was not Colonel Kurts in the movie, but in the eyes of the Hmong, he was bigger than life and could die or be killed.

Chapter 9

Cambodia- The Khmer Rouge

Cambodia came under Khmer rule around the 6th century, about the same time the Thai's began to migrate south from Southwest China and into Siam, know known as Thailand. In the 12th century the first Khmer's were Hindus. In 1863, the French colonized much of Southeast Asia, which included Cambodia, Vietnam and Laos into a single protectorate. Cambodia was a Monarchy which lasted until 1955 after the France gave Cambodia its independence in 1949 and pulled-out of Indochina in 1954. While war was raging in Vietnam, news reports concentrated on the events of the war in Vietnam and little attention was given to Cambodia's civil war. Cambodia was about the size of Missouri, with a population of 7.3 million and Laos only had 5 million people but Laos was important geographically for the United States in its campaign to stop the advancement of communism in Indochina and the use of the Ho Chi Minh Trail which crossed into Cambodia in the east. Cambodia was important to Thailand because it provided a buffer zone between Vietnam. Both Laos and Cambodia were waging its own war against communist insurgents ever since the French pulled out of Indochina. At least four communist groups were operating in Cambodia by 1970 and each promised the peasant farmers a better and prosperous society and a better way of life which failed to materialize.

The Viet Cong, and the NVA (North Vietnamese Army), were using Cambodia as a staging area for attacks against South Vietnam and American military installations. The U.S. began aerial bombing along the border of South Vietnam and Cambodia in an effort to disrupt the flow of supplies flowing down the Ho Chi Minh and Sihanouk trails as well as the Viet Cong encampments that were within the borders of Cambodia. The US bombing and American troops moving into the border areas played into the hands of the communist rhetoric about the invasion of the imperialist, and more and more recruits began believing the communist diatribe in Cambodia. One particular group was the Khmer Rouge, which was the radical extreme communist group who practiced the literal interpretation of Marxism with a twist of ancient Khmer past. Other communist groups were not as far right as the Khmer Rouge and had recruited mostly Vietnamese who were already communist that migrated out of South Vietnam when the Americans arrived in the early 1960's.

In 1941, King Norodom Sihanouk was coroneted as King of Cambodia after the death of King Sisowath Monivong. The French gave Cambodia its Independence in 1953, but two years later, Sihanouk abdicated his throne so he could form his own political party called Sangkum Political Party, for which he ran as Prime Minister. He named his father, Norodom Suramarit as King. When the elections were held in 1955, he was elected as Prime Minister of Cambodia. In 1960, his father, Norodom Suramarit died, and Sihanouk, introduced a Constitutional Amendment which made him Head of State of Cambodia.

Lon Nol's Regime

Lon Nol was born in 1913 in Cambodia from Chinese-Khmer descendants. He came from an affluent in Cambodia, where his father and grandfather both were Provincial Governors. He was educated in a prestigious school in Saigon and later graduated from the Cambodian Royal Military Academy. Prior to World War II, he became a Court Magistrate for the French Colonial Civil Service and after the War, served as Governor of Kratie Province. He joined the Cambodian Royal Army in 1952 and fought the Viet Minh for the French and later for King Norodom Sihanouk. After Cambodia's Independence in 1955, he became a key figure in King Sihanouk's Sangkum Party.

Lon Nol was Appointed Army Chief of Staff and Commander-in-Chief of the Army in 1955 by Sihanouk and in 1963 he was appointed Deputy Prime Minister. In 1966 he was elected Prime Minister while Sihanouk remained the self-appointed Head of State and declared Cambodia a neutral country. As years passed Sihanouk befriended the Communist and North Vietnamese who were using Cambodia's border areas as a staging area and supply route to assist the takeover of South Vietnam. He became friendly with Mao Zedong and North Korea, and began spending one and two month vacations in China and North Korea, where he built homes in both Beijing and North Korea.

The USA had been in a War with North Korea and now in Vietnam, so the relationship between Washington and Sihanouk had deteriorated to the point that in 1963 the USA cut foreign aid to Cambodia. Lon Nol on the other hand, was supportive to the United States, and had a long history of fighting the communist insurgence in Cambodia since the early 1950's. Nol and Sihanouk had a long standing hatred for the communist Marxist faction called the Khmer Rouge, however dismissed them as just another radical political group. Sihanouk made agreements with North Vietnam allowing them the use of the port in Phnom Penh as a supply depot for the Viet Cong fighting the Americans in South Vietnam. China's relationship with Russia had turned cold and that both countries cut-off diplomatic relations with each other and called back their Ambassadors and closed their Embassies.

In March of 1970, while Sihanouk was in Moscow, riots broke out in Phnom Penh by an anti-Vietnamese right wing groups who supported Lon Nol and Sirik Matak's anti-Communist policies. Lon Nol closed the port, which blocked the flow of weapons and supplies intended for the North Vietnamese Army and the Viet Cong. They also wanted the North Vietnamese and Viet Cong forces to withdraw from within the border areas of Cambodia within 72 hours. When the Vietnamese failed to respond to their request, US troops crossed into Cambodia and bombed and pushed the Viet Cong and North Vietnam Regulars north and into Laos.

A vote was taken in the National Assembly removing Sihanouk as Head of State and elected Lon Nol as the new Head of State. In October of 1970, the new Khmer Republic was declared. In the meantime, Sihanouk wasn't going down without a fight, so he formed GRUNK, (The Royal Government of National Union of Kampuchea), which was a consortium led by China, North Vietnam, North Korea, who's primary goal was to reinstate Sihanouk and boycotted the new regime of Lon Nol, and the new Khmer Republic Party. GRUNK, also allowed communist and Marist groups to join, perhaps from pressure by the communist governments, of which also included the Khmer Rouge Communist, under the leadership of Saloth Sar, later known as Pol Pot. Although, Sihanouk and the Khmer Rouge were bitter enemies and had fought each other over the past 20 years, he wanted to avenge Lon Nol and those who were responsible for his overthrow.

Sihanouk was vocal about accusing the United States, CIA for planning the coup. It was well established that Sihanouk was friendly with all of the communist countries and leaders and allowed the Viet Cong and Vietnamese troops to use Cambodia as a sanctuary to stage the fight against the Americans in South Vietnam. Lon Nol was pro American and Anti Communist, however, it was doubtful that the United States and the CIA were involved in the coup to replace Sihanouk.

Over the next few years, the Khmer Rouge controlled several regions near the Thai and Cambodian border. The Khmer Rouge gradually gained more support from the villages in the country side, partly because of the bombing of Cambodia, in which the Khmer Rouge seized on the opportunity use the bombing as an act of American imperialism.

In 1973, Sihanouk visited the Khmer Rouge strongholds in Cambodia and garnered popular support of the people. This made the Khmer Rouge uncomfortable, they believed that if they allied themselves with Sihanouk, their support for the Khmer Rouge may decline and the peasants would prefer to follow Sihanouk rather than the Khmer Rouge. The Khmer Rouge began a smear campaign against Sihanouk. The US Government warned Sihanouk that the Khmer Rouge was using him as a means to take control of the government and will discard him once they get into power. Sihanouk viewed American's concerns as "sour grapes".

As the Khmer Rouge's support grew in the country side, over the next few years the USA and Sihanouk felt that the Khmer Rouge was so radical in their Marxist beliefs that it would never take hold in Cambodia. It was dismissed as just another grass roots organization going nowhere. Most of the people who supported the Khmer Rouge thought that they were fighting to overthrow Lon Nol's government with the goal of installing Sihanouk's government back into power which is what the Khmer Rouge wanted the people to believe.

The key to recruitment for the Khmer Rouge is deception because if the people really knew what Marxist Communist demanded of its citizens, most people wouldn't support it. By spring of 1975, they had most of the support of rural Cambodians and were able to control most of the 5 million people in Cambodia. On April 17, 1975, the Khmer Rouge Army marched into Phnom Penh and took over the government with very little opposition. The Khmer Rouge took control of Sihanouk's GRUNK party while Sihanouk was vacationing in Pyongyang, North Korea. Most of the GRUNK party members were to be executed and Sihanouk was placed under house arrest when he returned from North Korea.

Years before, Lon Nol was appointed General of the Army because of his political connections more than his ability as a good military leader. He was a poor Presidential leader and many thought that he was not connected to the rural people of Cambodia, which made up most of the population. His primary interest was to destroy communist, and fight off his rivals. The economy in Cambodia had collapsed and he had no idea how to fix it. America didn't care about Cambodia's domestic and economic problems, as long as Lon Nol was continuing to fight communist insurgents, so in many respects the United States was using Lon Nol as a freedom fighter rather than a head of State. When the Khmer Rouge marched in Phnom Penh, Lon Nol fled to Indonesia and then to Hawaii, later he and his family would settle in California where he died of natural causes in 1985.

Saloth Sar, Alias Pol Pot

Saloth Sar was born in 1925 in a small village, 100 miles north of Phnom Penh. His family was affluent and he attended a Technical School in Paris in radio technology. It was while he was in Paris he became interested and active in Communism and in particular Marxism. He returned to Cambodia after school in 1954 when the French gave Cambodia its independence.

He joined the Khmer People's Revolutionary Party (KPRP) in 1954 while teaching French history and geography in a private school Phnom Penh until 1963. He continued to be active in the KPRP party and helped organize a group of pro-communist in 1960 who would met secretly at the railroad station in Phnom Penh. He decided to organize a new party called the "workers Party of Kampuchea" WPK for short. For the next thirteen years, the group vanished into the remote jungles of Cambodia and were seldom heard from or seen. He traveled occasionally to Beijing, China and Hanoi for organizational training and when he returned he once again changed the parties name to the "Communist Party of Kampuchea" for short, CPK.

As Vietnam was pulling out its forces in eastern Cambodia, Pol Pot's revolutionary army quickly replaced the Vietnamese military. For reasons unknown, Vietnam was increasingly becoming irritated with Pol Pot and his revolutionary forces. The Chinese provided five million dollars a year in weapons to his army which had grown to 35,000 regulars with 100,000 reserve troops. By 1973 the Khmer Rouge (CPK) controlled two-thirds of Cambodia and created cooperatives where the land was no longer privately owned in the northern regions and where controlled primarily by the Khmer Rouge.

When Phnom Penh fell to the Khmer Rouge in 1976, he renamed Cambodia "Democratic Kampuchea". In 1976, Sihanouk stepped down as Premier and Pol Pot became the new Premier of Democratic Kampuchea. Sihanouk had hoped to be part of the Khmer Rouge government but he remained under house arrest because of his popularity.

The Year Zero

Pol Pot declared "year zero" after the fall of Phnom Penh. He ordered the complete evacuation of Phnom

Penh and other towns and cities. He told the people that Phnom Penh was to be evacuated for their own safety; for fear that the Americans would bomb the cities. But in fact, he was sending them to collective farms to work and to purge anyone who was connected to the former Cambodia government and all immigrants and foreigners. Pol Pot also purged anyone who was a professional or intellectual, which include anyone who could spoke a second language, such as French or English. Keep in mind that Cambodia was a French colony and French was taught in Cambodia schools, so there were millions who spoke French as a second language. Pol Pot's goal was to cleanse Cambodia of all Ethnic races who were not of ancient Angkor Cambodian ancestry. It included: Ethnic Vietnamese, Chinese, Thai, and all religious groups including Catholics, Muslims and Buddhist Monks. The final group targeted for execution was the "Economic Saboteurs" who by Khmer's definition were the urban dwellers who lacked any agricultural ability. [30]

Some scholars and U.S. government officials claim the Khmer Rouge and Pol Pot were not communist, but rather a guerrilla organization that wanted the Viet Minh and foreigners out of the Cambodia. This of course was not necessarily true. Khmer Rouge's ideology was an extreme version Marxism based on Pol Pot's version of the ancient Khmer organization with Xenophobia tossed in, which became a recipe for genocide. [30]

By definition, Xenophobia is an intense or irrational dislike or fear of people from other countries or nationalities. This is often a characteristic common with dictators, but Pol Pot carried xenophobia to a new extreme.

S-21 and the Killing Fields

The Khmer Rouge created a special top secret prison which was a converted school in Phnom Penh, called S-21.

More than 16,000 prisoners were interrogated, tortured and murdered in the three years of its operation. It was under the supervision of Khang Khek Ieu, infamously known as "Comrade Duch".

Comrade Duch was a high school math teacher in Cambodia. His second in command was Comrade Chan, alias Mam Nai. He was also a high school teacher and well known by the prisoners as a "monster" who took special pleasure in torturing prisoners by using an electric wire.

The Chief of Security was Comrade Hor, alias Khem Vath who was well known for kicking prisoners to death. He would later be shot by Duch when the Khmer Rouge fled to the Thai-Cambodia border.

Comrade Peng was the Deputy Chief of Security and was known for his cruelty toward prisoners. He was also shot by Duch when they fled to the Thai-Cambodia border for reasons unknown.

Other notable cadres were Comrade Him Huy and Comrade Suos Thy. All but Comrade Duch escaped prosecution for war crimes. S-21 employed members of the Communists Youth League of Kampuchea who were between the ages of 12 to 21. It was patterned after the Revolutionary Red Guard during Mao's cultural revolution of the 1960's. Mao learned that youth were malleable and impressionable and could be directed to perform unspeakable crimes against prisoners and the general population without conscience. They were assigned tasks of transporting prisoners, torture, executions, interrogation and documentation. In the early 1980's, after Vietnam invaded Cambodia, many of the Khmer Rouge Revolutionary youths were rounded-up and arrested.

Pol Pot considered the Communist Youth League his most loyal and trusted members of the party and recruited them to spy on family members and anti-Angkor reactionaries that included almost everyone. They became enthusiastic accomplices to the regime and performed the worst atrocities. After most of the Youth Guard were arrested, many were brutally killed by local citizens who were victims of their rampage. **[Footnote 10]**

Comrade Duch Fig.12

Prisoners were taken to S-21 and forced to sign false confessions of alleged crimes for which they knew nothing of. The confessions were pre-prepared by security guards that claimed that the detainees were CIA operatives and spies for Vietnam and were disloyal to the Khmer Rouge. S-21 had a separate wing for women in which all were put to death. Children were taken to a separate detention center and killed.

The bodies were taken out of town and dumped into ditches and covered over. This would be known as the "Killing Fields". Only 14 people were known to survive S-21 prison when the Vietnamese Army marched into Phnom Penh in 1978. Those who did survive told of unspeakable horror that had taken place during their incarceration. The few that survived had special skills that were needed by the Khmer Rouge, such as carpenters, painters and technicians, which made up of 14 survivors. Foreigners from other countries were also victims. After lengthy and frequent torture, all would eventually sign confessions of guilt and were killed by pick-ax or other implements of death.

Babies were held up-side down and their skulls smashed against a large tree and their bodies tossed into a pit at the base of the "killing tree". Comrade Duch kept photos of each prisoner along with their confessions. Those he tortured and killed he failed to destroy the evidence of the atrocities when the Vietnamese invaded Cambodia in late 1978. Detainees were required to read the ten rules of the S-21 when they arrived. Failure to comply with the rules led to death by torture.

The Security Regulation (S-21)

1. *You must answer to my questions-Don't turn away.*

2. *Don't try to hide the facts by making pretexts this and that; you are strictly prohibited to contest me.*

3. *Don't be fool for you are a chap who dare thwart the revolution.*

4. *You must immediately answer questions without wasting time.*

5. *Don't tell me either about your immoralities or the essence of the revolution.*

173

6. *While getting lashes or electrification you must not cry at all*

7. *Do nothing, sit still and wait for my orders. If there is no order, keep quiet. When I ask you to do something, you must do it right away without protesting.*

8. *Don't make pretext about Kampuchea Kromin order to hide your secret traitor.*

9. *If you don't follow all the above rules, you shall get many lashes of electric wire.*

10. *If you disobey any point of my regulations you shall get either ten lashes or five shocks of electric discharge.*

Ten miles from S-21 was the killing fields where most of the bodies were buried. It was also the location where many were killed and buried. Bodies have also been found near S-21, which may have been the original location of disposing bodies until they had no room bury bodies and were forced to move to the forest outside of the city. In the 3 years of Pol Pot's rule, one quarter of the population of Cambodia had been exterminated. In a radio broadcast, the Khmer Rouge stated they only needed 1 to 2 million farmers in collectives to feed all of the people of Cambodia. It was during this period where the Khmer Rouge forced the educated, ethnic, foreigners, sick, elderly and those too young to work executed.

Before the take-over of the Khmer Rouge there were 500 licensed medical doctors in Cambodia, but a year later, there were only 40 remaining in Cambodia. Starvation was one of the methods of choice for murder by the Khmer Rouge, where they would burn down their homes and cut all of the fruit trees, and destroy food and crops and prohibited fishing or going into the jungle to forage or planting. Eating wild berries was punishable by death. They would slowly starve entire families and villages to death. It has been estimated that hundreds of thousands were killed in this manner.

S-21 prison in Phnom Penh Fig 13

Certain groups were classified as "Depositees", and were moved from the urban City of Phnom Penh, and forced to march to rural communes for manual hard labor. "Depositees" were those who had no farming skills and were considered a burden on society. Most were marked for death as soon as they were no longer needed after the harvest.

Many were forced to dig their own graves and were buried alive. Asian pick axes were common tool used on farms in which the Khmer Rouge used to murder people. In the early years of Khmer rule, they stabbed the victims in neck with a ice pick which was the method most often used in S-21 prison. The Khmer government refused humanitarian aid, because accepting meant that their brand of Communist wasn't working. While Cambodians were being starved by the thousands, Pol Pot's Regime was exporting thousands of tons of rice, weekly to build the treasury of the Khmer Rouge government, while little if any was given to the workers in the communes or collectives. This was a common practice used by other communist leaders such as Mao Zedong and Kim Il-sung of North Korea.

Pol Pot always remained in the shadows and was rarely seen in public. Unlike other dictators such as Mao Zedong, Stalin, Kim IL Sung, Pol Pot did not have a "cult personality" and remained anonymous during most of his rule. Very few people knew who the leader of Cambodia was. When the Vietnamese invaded Cambodia in 1978, they found more than 20,000 mass graves throughout Cambodia with an estimated 1.7 to 2 million people killed under Pol Pot's Khmer Rouge regime.

Pol Pot's down fall came when tensions with Vietnam deteriorated due to a series of border clashes between Vietnam and Cambodia. Cambodia invaded deep into South Vietnam in an effort to "take back" territory lost to Vietnam centuries earlier. There were claims that the Khmer Rouge practiced genocide on the Vietnamese who lived along the border of Vietnam and Cambodia. More than 100,000 Cambodian/Vietnamese were killed as a means of retaliating against Vietnam.

It was the final straw for Vietnam, and they attacked with full force and defeated the Khmer Rouge in the matter of weeks and marched into the capital of Phnom Penh to take control. Pol Pot and the Khmer Rouge, along with Sihanouk, fled to the Thai border, out of harm's way of the Vietnamese. The USA and China had a personal vendetta against Vietnam and elected to support Pol Pot and the Khmer Rouge in an effort to reinstall Pol Pot back into power. The U.S.A. provided 17 million dollars a year in covert aid to the Khmer Rouge insurgents and China gave the Khmer Rouge an additional 100 million dollars. Thailand became the secret go between in which money and weapons were funneled to the Khmer Rouge from Thailand. China and America wanted the Khmer Rouge to gain military strength and push the Vietnamese out of Cambodia. The USA voted in the UN, recognizing the Khmer Rouge and the Pol Pot's Regime as the only legitimate Government of Cambodia.

While the Vietnamese Army occupied Cambodia, they allowed Cambodia to establish its own government, which was run by former members of Sihanouk's and Lon Nol's government. It was called the "People's Republic of Kampuchea", which would become a dictatorship, under the Vietnamese installed puppet ruler, Hun Sun.

A Policy of Hatred

Since the start of the Vietnam War in 1962, the United States saw South Vietnam and Laos fall to communism, and feared that Cambodia would be the next. When Vietnamese marched into Cambodia in 1978, both the United States and China believed that Vietnam wanted to expand its borders. After decades of fighting, it had become an organized military power in Southeast Asia. It also acquired a large arsenal of American military arms and equipment left behind after the fall of South Vietnam. Vietnam was the most populous county in Indochina, with nearly 80 million people, while Cambodia had only 8 million people.

China was having border clashes with Vietnam, in which both sides claimed victory over the other, but the invasion of Cambodia brought disdain to China and the United States. Vietnam claimed that Cambodia used genocide against the Vietnamese and other ethnic groups, and sent raiding parties into South Vietnam and burned entire villages and killing most of the inhabitants. The

United States had a vendetta against Vietnam as a result of South Vietnam's repeated violations of the Paris Peace agreement. China was concerned over Vietnam's growing military strength and being closely allied with the Soviet Union, in which China's relationship with Russia had turned sour over China's border clashes with Russia.

In 1979, the United States and China voted in the UN General Assembly granting Cambodia a UN seat to the ousted Khmer Rouge Regime and terminated any UN investigation into Khmer Rouge's crimes against humanity. The United States cut-off all humanitarian aid to Cambodia's current government under Hun Sun, who was the President of Cambodia. Pol Pot and the Khmer Rouge fled to the jungles near the border of Thailand and Cambodia. [31]

In 1985, Vietnam negotiated a plan for the withdrawal from Cambodia with the condition that the Khmer Rouge be excluded from holding any positions of power within the government. China and the United States rejected the terms of the agreement. In 1989, UNICEF reported that 20% of the Cambodian children were suffering from malnutrition but no aid was being sent due to objections by Japan and the United States. The Red Cross estimated that 80% of the Red Cross and UN food aid was actioned off before being receive by the Cambodian refugees. [31]

During the Paris Peace talks, the Cambodian Government and Vietnamese delegation insisted that any newly installed government after Vietnam pulls out of Cambodia should not have a prior history of past practices of genocide and must have free elections. The Chinese and Khmer Rouge guerrilla army delegation insisted that the years the Khmer Rouge was in power from 1975 to 1978, they did not practice genocide, while United States maintained that the Khmer Rouge actions "did not fit the legal definition of genocide". The United States, Great Britain, France and Japan agreed, and the language was stricken from the proposed agreement. This would clear the way for Pol Pot's and his communist Khmer Rouge to return. [31] **[Footnote 11]**

In a coalition with China, the United States guaranteed Pol Pot immunity from his crimes against humanity and genocide between the years of 1975 to 1978 by drafting a peace plan in the UN and dropping all mention of "Genocide" and replacing the term with "Euphemism". The UN Human Rights Commission in 1991 publicly drafted a resolution which stated,

"...the atrocities reaching the level of genocide committed in particular during the period of Khmer Rouge rule.... detect, arrest, extradite or bring to trial those who have been responsible for crimes against humanity in Cambodia". [29]

Vietnam withdrew its troops in 1989 and the Cambodian Government remained under the leadership of Hun Sun. The Khmer Rouge rebels eventually disbanded and denounce the Khmer Rouge cause and supported the Vietnamese installed Cambodian Government of Hun Sun. Pol Pot and the Khmer Rouge failed to take over the Cambodian government that was supported by President's Jimmy Carter, Ronald Reagan and George HW Bush. [29]

As Jack Wheeler stated, *".....there are eight anti-Soviet guerrilla wars being conducted in the third world at this moment....sooner or later, one of these movements is going to win.... The first successful over throw of a Soviet puppet regime may, in fact, precipitate a reverse domino effect, a toppling of Soviet dominos one after the other."* [32]

But to the millions of Cambodian families who lost their loved ones, and the memories of Pol Pot and the Khmer Rouge, will be never forget, as long as justice for those who committed crimes against humanity go unpunished and remain protected against prosecution.

The denial of food and medical aid to those that remained behind in Cambodia under Hun Sun's regime also became victims. Thousands died of starvation when humanitarian aid and monetary credit was denied by the International Monetary Fund. Pol Pot and the Khmer Rouge were being generously supplied with food and money until Pol Pot's death. He was convicted of war crimes in absentia and given the death penalty, but died while in hiding in the jungles of Cambodia. Only four of the leaders of the Khmer Rouge has ever been charged and convicted of their crimes by a joint judicial French and Cambodian trial. The trial was held in July of 2010, 35 years later. The United States elected not get involved in the trial as a result of their support for Pol Pot and the Khmer Rouge. The Hollywood movie; "The Killing Fields" opened in theaters in November of 1984, which brought the reality of the crimes perpetrated by the Khmer Rouge to the American public.

During an ABC News special broadcast in April 26, 1990, Rep. Chester Atkins (Dem Mass.) was asked what the US policy in Cambodia is. He replied; *"A policy of hatred"*.

Chapter 10

The Sino-Vietnam War

Few people were aware that America came close to a third world war in Asia shortly after the Vietnam invaded Cambodia in 1979. Surprisingly, America had a fear that China and the Soviet Union may become involved in the Vietnam War as a result of America's combat role in Southeast Asia, which was not the case. Soon after the last U.S. troops left Vietnam, Pol Pot and the Khmer Rouge had taken over Lon Nol's Cambodian regime in 1976, and war between, Cambodia, Thailand, Vietnam and China broke-out in the form of minor border skirmishes. It would be precipitate into a full conflict in 1979. In Chapter 7 and 8, I briefly mentioned the relationship between China and Vietnam which had soured as a result of a border dispute with China; however, the border clashes intensified from minor skirmishes in 1979 to full scale battle by 1986.

Vietnam was having border clashes with Cambodia in December 1978, which prompted Vietnam to deployed 180,000 troops with heavy armored into Cambodia. In the interim, China tried to mediate talks between Vietnam and Cambodia to resolve issues concerning their border disputes, but talks stalled. Vietnam elected to take military action against Cambodia.

North Vietnam had a sizeable army capable of defending two fronts; Cambodia in the South and China in the North. Minor border clashes continued along both fronts. China took advantage of the situation in Cambodia and deployed more than 80,000 troops and 400 tanks into the northern border of Vietnam. They advanced as far south as 15 miles into North Vietnam. Vietnam deployed more than 50,000 regular troops and 75,000 reserve troops to stop the Chinese (PLA) advance.

The Chinese Army crossed into Laos, perhaps for the purpose of securing more real-estate or for a defensive position. The territory that China occupied had no strategic value to China and no clear reason for China to seize land since it only involved an area of 23 square miles, but Vietnam would defend the invasion regardless.

As a result of failed negotiations with China, Vietnam signed a military Pac with the Soviet Union to supply military aid and equipment to Vietnam should the conflict escalate into war. Vietnam allowed the Soviets to construct a port facility in Cam Ranh Bay in Vietnam which surprised U.S officials. China was allies to Thailand and the Khmer Rouge when the Vietnamese Army in Cambodia attacked a Khmer Rouge camp in Thailand, which put the Thai military on alert and prompted China to launch a heavy artillery barrage in June of 1980 on the Cao Bang Province in North Vietnam. In May of 1981, fierce fighting erupted in the Cao Loc and Lang Son Province of Vietnam which claimed numerous casualties on both sides. In retaliation, Vietnam forces attacked the Guangxi and Yunnan Provinces in China with heavy losses on both sides. This "tit for tat" would continue for years.

The Battle of Laoshan

The bloodiest battle of the conflict occurred on April 2, 1984 in the Northern Provinces of Lang Son, Cao Bang, Ha Tuyen and Hoang Len Son. The Chinese Army (PLA) attacked 16 Northern Provinces with a barrage of 60,000 heavy artillery rounds followed by a ground assault in an effort to secure the hills and highlands. The battle continued for 26 days in which the PLA fell back and held a 2 mile border area inside Vietnam. The casualties were heavy on both sides, but the PLA sustained slightly more casualties than the Vietnamese Army (VPA).

In 1986 and 1987, the Chinese fired 800,000 rounds of artillery into the border area and in particular Vi Xuyen district, which was heavily fortified by the VPA. The PLA launched several major attacks on Vietnamese positions but were repelled. On October 5, 1987, the Chinese shot down a Vietnamese Mig 21 fighter over Guangxi Province in China. Small skirmishes continued throughout 1986 and 1987. Soviet President, Mikhail Gorbachev made a request to normalize relationships between Vietnam and China to stabilize peace in Indochina, but China insisted that negotiations would require Vietnam to pull-out of Cambodia before peace talks could begin. Vietnam refused the offer and the war continued. On March 14, 1988, a naval battle between China and Vietnam was fought over the Spratly Islands off the coast of Vietnam, in which 64 Vietnamese soldiers were killed. The conflict over the Spratly Islands continues today.

In response to international condemnation of Vietnam's invasion of Cambodia, in 1988, Vietnam began to pull-out troops from Cambodia. By September 1989 the remaining 26,000 troops left Cambodia. But in keeping with past history of broken agreements, in 1991, Vietnamese troops were spotted entering the Kampot Province of Cambodia. The border war with China resulted in the Chengdu Summit in which China and Vietnam normalized relations in November of 1991. As a concession, Vietnam ceded a small piece of border real-estate.

The actual number killed during the Sino-Vietnam war was estimated to be 10,000 Chinese and an unknown number of Vietnamese, which no one will admit too.

Vietnam claimed they lost 23,000 killed and 55,000 wounded in the ten years in Cambodia. The number of civilian deaths in the Sino-Vietnamese War may have been as many as 100,000.

The final conclusion was that the Sino-Vietnam war had no clear winners. China got the Spratly Islands, and a small territory along the border of Vietnam. Vietnam pulled-out of Cambodia and China didn't get the Khmer Rouge back in power. The Soviet Union became a democracy and Vietnam lost its only ally, who provided $1.2 billion in military aid to Vietnam. Most of the Chinese who resided in Vietnam were exiled.

For the invasion of Cambodia, Vietnam thought they would get praise for ousting Pol Pot, the communist dictator known for his atrocities. However, the opposite was the case. The entire international community looked upon Vietnam as the aggressor and in fact said nothing to China when they invaded North Vietnam. It would cost Vietnam its membership in the Asian Development Bank and the International Monetary Fund. Foreign investment in Vietnam dried up and they were experiencing serious financial problems, especially after being in war for more than 50 years. It had become a war machine rather than an economic system of development and became the fifth largest Army in the World, yet it became one of the poorest countries in the World. It wasn't until 1991 when the last of the remains of American troops were returned to the United States and Vietnam's exit from Cambodia that the United States normalized trade relations with Vietnam, however limited.

On November 14, 1991 elections were scheduled to take place in Cambodia. Sihanouk, the former Cambodian official and Son Senn arrived in Phnom Penh to setup a campaign office. On November 27th former head of the Khmer Rouge, Khieu Samphan, arrived in Phnom Penh from Bangkok but was met by an angry crowd which turned into a mob. As Samphan made a dash to his office, the mob broke into his building and chased him to the second floor and tried to hang him from a ceiling fan, but he managed to escape by climbing down a fire exit ladder to a waiting vehicle that took him to the airport. His political career was short lived, especially if the mob was able to catch him. He would later receive a life sentence for crimes against humanity for his role in the Khmer Rouge. [80]

To this day, Khieu Samphan continues to claim that the millions he ordered killed were enemies of the State and received just punishment.

Chapter 11

Thailand and Burma

Thai's were part of the Thai Kadai ethnic group from Southwest China who migrated south in the 6th century. They had a long history of conflict with the Shan Burmese and the Khmer Cambodians throughout history. Thailand was never colonized as other Southeast Asian countries had been, but in 1824, the British established a colonial foothold in the teak trade in northern Thailand, which lasted until 1896 with an agreement that guaranteed Thailand's (Siam at the time) independence. In 1932, Thailand established a representative democracy and a constitutional Monarchy and changed the name from Siam to Thailand.

Thailand is definitely a land of contrast, not especially geographically, but also politically. It is a country in constant turmoil and transition. But even when there is a change in government, on the average every four years, nothing seems to bother the Thai people, and in most cases one wouldn't even notice that there had been a change at all, it's always business as usual for the rural and general population.

On December 8, 1941, one day after the bombing of Pearl Harbor in Hawaii, Japan invaded Thailand. The Prime Minister, Plaek Phibunsongkhram (Phibun), ordered a cease fire after a few skirmishes. Japan and Thailand signed a pact, in which Japan would have full access to all of the military bases, railroads, roads and communications and essential government buildings and warehouses, yet Phibun would continue to run the Thai Government. [33]

On January 25, 1942, Thailand declared war on Britain and the United States, but the Thai Ambassador to Washington DC elected not to give the declaration of war to the Secretary of State and President Roosevelt, so technically they were not at war with the United States. [33]

While the war continued in the Pacific, on December 1, 1942, the Communist Party of Thailand (CPT) became an official party and was actively recruiting supporters in rural Thailand, mostly in the northeast. Prior to that period, it was known as the Communist Party of Siam, which had roots as far back as the late 1920's. [34]

During World War II, the communist party activities remained somewhat stalled, partly because of Phibun, who became Minister of Defense in 1934. Phibun had a career in the Military and attended the Military Academy and rose to the rank of Major before becoming Defense Minister. He became Prime Minister in December of 1938 and presided over a cabinet of twenty five members, of which fifteen were military personnel. Phibun ran his government as an authoritarian or military organization, which was one reason why the communist had difficulty taking hold during his reign from 1938 to 1944. [35]

Phibun's popularity among the people began to deteriorate, as Japan wanted more and more concessions from Thailand, and it was clear that Japan was losing the war. Since Thailand had never been colonized, they did not want Japan to colonize Thailand after the war. Many accused Phibun of being pro Japanese, but more than likely, he wanted to protect the people and Thailand from the effects of war and especially as a conquered nation. By 1944, Japan was clearly on the verge of falling to the allies, as did Hitler in Europe.

The allies had liberated France in 1944 and Italy had executed Mussolini, so Italy was no longer a factor in the war. Thailand thought it best to distance itself from Japan as soon as it became obvious that they were losing the war. It was mutually agreed upon by the Thai government that Phibun had to be replaced due to his perceived war time connection with Japan. On August 1, 1944, Khuang Aphaiwong was appointed Prime Minister of Thailand but would only remain in office for only one year. [35]

The Death Railroad

During World War II, the Japanese advanced into the West Indies, Singapore, Malaysia, Thailand and Burma. As a result of the invasion they had taken many Dutch, Australian and British prisoners who had colonized most of the Dutch West Indies and Malayan Peninsula as part of the British and Dutch colonies. When the Japanese invaded Burma, the British moved its troops into India to make a stand against the Japanese. The British troops were under the command of Lord Mountbatten, who had recruited a sizeable army of Gurkhas from Nepal and a large Indian/British Army from India to hold off the Japanese advance into India.

The Japanese tried to advance a large army from Thailand into the jungles of Burma but lost most of its army became stricken with tropical disease, starvation and exhaustion. The army couldn't carry enough military equipment and supplies on their backs in the Jungle to mount a formidable military campaign against the British, who were holding-out in the jungles of Northern Burma and the border areas of India.

The Japanese decided the only option was to complete a railroad from Rangoon, Burma to Bangkok, Thailand. Part of the railroad had already built, but 258 miles remained to be constructed which was in the most uninhabitable jungle and mountainous terrain along on the railroad corridor. They would need to construct 600 bridges and cross over the Three Pagoda Pass on the border of Burma and Thailand. It would require about 250,000 laborers and 12,000 Japanese and Korean Engineers and Soldiers.

Work began in June of 1942. One group started on the Burmese side and another on the Thailand side. More than 60,000 prisoners of war from Singapore, Malaysia, Burma and Indonesia we transported to camps along the Railroad corridor, north of Bangkok and South of Rangoon, Burma. 180,000 Asia workers, mostly from Burma and Thailand also worked on the railroad, of which, half would die of starvation and disease.

There were virtually no medical facilities available, just a few clinics for the prisoners and only a half cup of rice for food per day. Malaria, dysentery, plague and infections began to take a huge toll on the prisoners and Asian laborers. By the time the railroad was completed (1 ½ years later) in December of 1943, 12,621 allied prisoners had died, which include, British, Dutch, Australians and a few Americans. More than 90,000 Asian laborers would also die. The total death toll was over 100,000 deaths. For those who did survive, they reminisce about the torture and mistreatment they endured. While many Japanese Commanders were reasonably fair, however there were some that were unusually cruel to the prisoners.

At the end of the war, 111 Japanese and Koreans were tried as war criminals for their inhumane treatment and brutality toward prisoners of war while constructing the death railroad. Thirty-two were sentenced to death. In the City of Kanchanaburi, Thailand a memorial called the "Garden of the Buried" of the many that gave their lives to the construction of the railroad. A museum was built to honor those who worked and died on the railroad. It sits at the bridge entrance on the River Kwai Yai.

War Reparation

At the end of the War, Great Britain demanded war reparation from Thailand as a result of colluding with the Axis powers and because of their declaration of war against Great Britain. Britain gave Thailand a long list of remedies as war reparations. Thailand declared that the declaration of War by Phibun was illegal because it lacked specific signatures from the Council of Regency. The United States came to Thailand's defense and claimed that Thailand was a puppet government like France and any war reparation by Britain should be reconsidered. Great Britain compromised. Four years later, Phibun became Prime Minister again which he held that position until 1957. [35]

The reason this part of Thai history is important, is to understand the background in American and Thailand's relationship and their involvement in the war against communism in Asia, and later the war against drugs. Because of those circumstances in history, Asia may have been a much different place to live had Thailand fallen to communism like Laos, Cambodia and Vietnam.

Thailand's War on Communism

Thailand and America's relationship prior to 1948 was only extended to the trade of tin and rubber, or at least until the Japanese invaded Thailand in 1941, in which trade ended completely at that point.

With Mao Zedong's victory in China in 1949 and the Korean War in 1950 and the French fighting the Viet Minh in Vietnam, the United States was afraid that the "domino effect" of communism would spread throughout Southeast Asia and into the Philippines and even as far as Australia. The United States needed an ally in Southeast Asia for which to launch an offensive from. The United States also need to build air bases and ports to bring in military supplies and equipment in to Asia, should it be necessary. As a result of America aiding Thailand after the war, Phibun, now Prime Minister again, was more than happy to accommodate the United States. He also disliked communist, which represented a threat to Thailand, since it was apparent that most of Southeast Asia may eventually fall under communist control. America and Thailand's relationship became a symbiotic relationship.

Burma, Thailand Railroad, built 1943 Fig 15

The United States from 1951 to 1957 provided Thailand with 149 million dollars in economic aid and 222 million dollars in military aid. Thailand was the first Southeast Asian country to send troops to Korea and fight against the North Koreans in 1951. During the Vietnam War, Thailand was active in fighting communist insurgents in Cambodia, Vietnam and Laos. Thailand sent more than

191

121,000 troops into Laos to fight Pathet Laos and Viet Minh communist insurgents. The United States was forbidden under the Geneva Convention to participate in fighting in Laos, so Thailand troops dressed in Loa Nationalist military uniforms help fight the secret war in Laos. [37]

Many of the Pathet Laos Communist had moved into the Northeast of Thailand in the mountainous region of Loei, and on the border of Laos and Thailand. It is one of the most remote areas in Thailand, but easy access to a well maintained road system. The Communist Party of Thailand (CPT) had increased its ranks as a result of the Pathet Laos moving south and joining forces with the CPT in the mountains of Loei.

The CPT would conduct guerrilla raids in both Thailand and Laos while using Thailand as its base of operations, while Thai troops were in Laos fighting communist insurgents from North Vietnam. The one problem with the Loei mountain hold-out was that Phibun's anti-communist troops could keep the CPT and Pathet Laos confined to a relatively small mountainous region far from any large population center.

Any movement out of the Loei Region and into the "Esan Plateau" (e-son) would be easily detected by the Thai military, and they would be "sitting ducks" against a vastly superior well equipped force. To complicate the situation even further for CPT, the United States and Thailand built a large military installation in Udon Thani (Udon), which was the headquarters for the CIA in Southeast Asia. The United States Air Force and the Thai Army was located in Udon Thani. In addition, the 10,000 foot runway accommodated B-52 bombers which were used to bomb Hanoi and the Ho Chi Minh trail and the Plain of Jars in Laos. The Thai troops were also based at Udon Thani as well. Udon Thani was located only 35 miles south of Loei and 25 miles from the Laos border. This was the worst possible situation for CPT, because a helicopter flying recon could detect the insurgent's hideout in Loei Mountains while on coffee break, making sure that they hadn't moved, so in essence, they were pinned down and could only move at night.

In 1966, US intelligent reports indicated that Beijing agents had infiltrated hill tribe villages in both Laos and Thailand and was sponsoring and recruiting for the CPT. It was also reported that there was a connection between Beijing and the Muslim insurgency in Southern Thailand. It was believed that while Thai troops were busy fighting Muslim insurgents in Southern Thailand, it would take pressure off the Pathet Laos and CPT in the Northeast of Thailand.

The ideology of the CPT was a Marxist-Lenin theory of Communism in which Beijing wanted the United States out of Thailand and in fact, out of Asia entirely. With the US withdrawal from Thailand, Beijing hoped that military support from the United States to fight communism would dry up. Beijing's goal was to pressure governments and cause citizen insurrection about the presence of a foreign power in their country. If the communist could get rid of the United States, it would have clear a path for a communist take-over of Southeast Asia and especially Thailand.

Beijing also feared that the United States would establish permanent military presences and bases in Thailand to fight communism, which was the worst option for the communist. They also thought that there was no need to fight the US directly, but rather infiltrate and create a propaganda campaign among the local Thai's about US occupation, causing protests and riots. All this effort on behalf of the insurgents failed to materialize and to get much support in Thailand, partly because Thailand was fearful that the communism would take-over as they had in other Asian countries and their loyalty to King and the Thai Monarch would be compromised under communism which was completely unacceptable to the Thai people.

In 1967, Washington approved 71 million dollars for Thailand to purchase more helicopters to fight insurgents in Northeastern Thailand and to create the "Communist Suppression Operation Command". During a 1969 Senate hearings, it was revealed that Thai Special Forces had dressed up as Laos's and Hmong tribesmen and infiltrated into Laos to fight communist insurgents and provide clandestine operations, which was apparently successful by all accounts. [37]

Communist insurgents in Thailand were not a successful program for Beijing as it had been in Laos and Vietnam and Cambodia.

Thailand was one of the most prosperous countries in Southeast Asia and even though over 40 percent of the people were poor and rural farmers, they were still better off than the neighboring countries. The Thais owned their own land and were able to trade freely under a capitalist system. Converting an entire population to communism was not an option for the Thai people. Regardless who was running the government at the time, it was well established that the government always treated its citizens well and had an undying loyalty to its King and Queen. After the Vietnam War in 1975, the Thai government offered amnesty to those who were Thai Communist, who were holding-out in the Loei Region in Esan and other enclaves. Almost all of the Thai communist insurgents accepted the governments offer. It was one of the biggest success stories of the Vietnam War era.

Burma: Sixty Years of Oppression

Burma was a colony of Great Britain from 1824 to 1948. It was one of the more affluent societies in Asia, but after World War II, Burma gained its independence and formed a bicameral parliament and installed its first President and Prime Minister. For the next 14 years, thing were going well for Burma until it built a military machine without adequate oversight and control by the civilian government. It was just a matter of time before an ambitious General would seize control of the government in a Coup d'état using the military to accomplish the goal.

General Ne Win

As mentioned, Burma was doing well economically until March of 1962 when General Ne Win took control of Burma under a coup d'état.

Shortly after taking power he formed the Burma Socialist Program Party (BSPP) which was a form of Communist Marxism with a twist of Buddhism thrown in. It was the only legal party allowed in the country, so he had no opposition. In 1974, he formed the Socialist Republic of the Union of Burma in which he declared himself President, and appointed General Sein Win as Prime Minister. In 1972, he expelled all foreigners and restricted foreign visitors to a to 3 day visa, in which he later increased the visa requirement to 5 days.

General Ne Win was of Chinese ancestry, but for some unknown reason, he developed a disdain toward the Chinese. In 1963, he passed the Enterprise Nationalization Law, which nationalized all major industry and factories in Burma, which by definition would be Fascism. Other laws were passed that prohibited foreigners and non-citizen Chinese from owning land, businesses and practicing medicine. [79] More than 100,000 Chinese left Burma in exile. He wasn't content with exiling a few hundred thousand Chinese, so he banned Chinese-language education and orchestrated an anti-Chinese propaganda campaign which started riots in 1967 that continued through 1970. It was a form of ethnic and racial cleansing of Chinese.

He was a strong believer in numerology and astrology and would only print money (kyat) in denominations that were devisable by the number 9 and would add up to 9; such as 45 and 90. He once went to a monk to foresee his future, and the Monk told him there would be a massive up-rising and bloodshed and many would die. He went home, looked into the mirror, threw a piece of meat on the floor and began jumping and stomp on it, then he took his revolver from his holster, and shot at the image of himself in the mirror, which he hoped would stop any possible assassination attempts on his life during the revolt.

Riots continued from 1965 to 1970. At one point the Universities were closed for two years. In 1988, pro-democracy riots broke-out again in Rangoon, which was known as the 'Four Eights Uprising' which forced Ne Win to resign from the BSPP Congress. In 2002, while under house arrest for an alleged coup d'état conspiracy, he died with little notice in the newspaper, and only 30 people were allowed to attended his funeral. In 1989, the government changed the name of Burma to the "Union of Myanmar".

Riots continued until the government ordered the military to fire upon the demonstrators, killing and wounding as many as 3,000. General Than Shwe would become the head of the 'State Law and Order Restoration Council' and Commander in Chief of the Myanmar Armed Forces. The country was ruled for the next four years by another military dictator and fascist.

In the spring of 1990, under pressure from the United States and World opinion, elections were held in which the National League of Democracy won 80% of the seats in Parliament, and named Aung San Suu Kyi as Prime Minister. However, the military junta did not cede power and instead placed Aung San Suu Kyi under house arrest as a political prisoner. Over the next 21 years, she would remain under house arrest until 2011. She was awarded the Nobel Prize for Peace in 1991 in her efforts to reform and bring free elections and democracy to Burma.

General Than Shwe took power in 1992. Ne Win left a legacy of bankrupting a nation, and Than Shwe's first goal was to orchestrate some form of fiscal responsibility.

Since he was a military dictator, his first goal was to build a massive military machine, construct a new capital and build an army of over 400,000 troops which was costing the government 40% of its annual budget. Most of the manufacturing was shut down with the expelling of the Chinese which plunged the country into near bankruptcy. He relaxed state controls over the economy and targeted corruption in the military and police, but to no success.

In 2004, he was responsible for the removal of Khin Nyunt, the Prime Minister, which gave him virtually unlimited control and power in the government. He suppressed free press, free speech and the detention of journalist who opposed his regime. He censored newspapers, television and radio programming. Tourist were not allowed to bring movie cameras into the country and visitors had to be escorted by government security guards to insure that only sites acceptable to the government were visited. It was the most repressive regime in Asia with the exception of North Korea.

In 2007, a mass Buddhist monk demonstration was staged in Yangon, called the "Saffron Revolution", to protest the incarceration of political prisoners and gross human rights violations, but was met by security forces that fired directly into the crowds, killing hundreds of protesters and monks. Some claim as many as 1,000 were arrested and taken into the jungle and executed, but because of government censorship, it is difficult to confirm the actual number arrested and imprisoned and killed. Many were buried alive in shallow graves and drowned in the river, as survivors and eye witnesses claim. This type of military executions was common in Myanmar ever since becoming a military dictatorship.

Naypyidaw, Myanmar's New Capital

There is a lot of speculation by foreign governments concerning why General Than Shwe elected to move the capital 200 miles north of Yangon to Naypyidaw, which was in the middle of nowhere, especially, shortly after becoming the self appointed leader of Myanmar, in which the country was on the verge of bankruptcy. But it is my belief that it was moved because of the frequent riots and demonstration of millions of Burmese protesting military control of the government over the last 20 years. General Than Shwe believed that at anytime the capital in Yangon could be taken over by the people by storming the central power of government in Yangon, as so many other governments have fallen in this way. He built a huge military complex in the new capital, obviously for the protection of the central capital of Naypyidaw and for his self protection.

Burma today is still a Military dictatorship, under the guise of Democracy and for the first time in 65 years, Myanmar has a civilian President, albeit his or her power and authority is limited and in constant threat of military control to thwarts any real change. The Constitution cannot be changed because 25% of Parliament is military and constitutional change requires 76%. So, as I have said before; the more things change the more they stay the same. Burma is a beautiful country that has been damaged by ruthless leaders that has suppressed the basic rights of humanity towards its people. It is still a country that is 50 to 75 years behind in technology and the basic conveniences that Thailand and other Southeast Asian countries enjoy today. All this is the result of hate and greed.

Chapter 12

Indonesia and Singapore

Indonesia is comprised of 17,000 islands with hundreds of different indigenous beliefs and religions, which has proved to be a difficult task in making Indonesia a homogenous nation. Hindu was brought to the islands by traders in the first and second centuries and the Muslim in the 13th century. Most of the archipelago had converted to Islam by the 15th century.

The Portuguese traders arrived in the 14th century and the Dutch in the 16th century. The British seized the islands in 1811 but returned them back to the Dutch in 1816. In 1922, Indonesia was made part of the Dutch Kingdom but after World War II, Sukarno and Mohammed Hatta declared Indonesia as an independent nation and has been ever since.

Indonesia and the Philippines had a great deal in common in the early years. They both are island nations, neighbors, ruled by dictators, anti-communist and both have the dubious distinction of being among the most corruption governments of all time. Both Philippines and Indonesia were supported by the United States.

Although, there were governments in the past and present that served their country and people well in both Indonesia and the Philippines, however two dictators in particular drove their country into debt by diverting billions of dollars into their personal off shore accounts while the entire country lived in poverty. Because of corruption, they were well known for their human rights violations, torture, murder and imprisonment of political opposition.

Indonesia

During World War II, the Japanese approached Mohammad Hatta Sukarno about using Indonesia as a base of operations in Southeast Asia. It was a Dutch colony and Sukarno was the quasi President of the colony. He was a socialist but was well respected by the people of Indonesia. He negotiated a deal with the Japanese to provide fuel oil and rubber and goods to Japan during the war in exchange for Japan giving Indonesia its independence from the Netherlands after the war.

By 1945, Japan was losing the war, and the Americans had taken Okinawa, however, Sukarno announced that Indonesia as an independent Republic on August 17, 1945, just fifteen days before the official signing of the surrender of Japan.

Sukarno became the first President of Indonesia, however he was a socialist and had his own brand of Marxism, called, "Marhaenism", which was a play on words for Marxism and Indonesia, a mix of communism adjusted for Indonesian culture. A constitution was written and a Parliament was established, but almost immediately, problems surfaced due to the differences in religion, social and ethnic composition of Indonesia.

There were 17,000 islands and each had their own traditional language and lifestyle and religion. Over the next five years, there were continued insurrection, murders, kidnappings and attempted coups. He was desperate to find a solution and realized that "Marhaenism" wasn't going to work. So he designed a political system called "Guided Democracy" which in effect was nothing more than a combination of fascism and communism patterned after the Germany in the 1930's and Marxism in Russia.

Guided Democracy

Sukarno came up with a new political government which would take into account Indonesia's traditional and religious principles, called, "Guided Democracy". As warm and fuzzy as it sounded, it was nothing more than Communism with a false expectation of democracy. He built the "Peoples Security Army" which was equivalent to the Nazi's Brown Shirts, and became dependent on the Communist Party of Indonesia (PKI) to obtain aid from Russia. By early 1950's, Sukarno appointed more and more communist in his government, much to the disapproval of the United States.

Even though Sukarno was building up a communist government, seven of his top military generals, including Major General Nasution, who was Sukarno's second in command, were staunch anti-communist. In 1958, the rebel group PRRI was formed, which included anti-communist and Islamic rebels. The arms and financial aid was provided by England, America and Australia. The CIA was heavily involved in Indonesia's politics but denied everything. There were several attempts on Sukarno's life in 1956, but he still had a firm grip on the government and surprisingly was very popular among the people.

Allen Lawrence Pope Incident

Pope was a retired US Air Force pilot who flew during the Korean War and the Vietnam War when the French occupied Vietnam. In 1954, the CIA recruited him to fly C-119 Flying Boxcars for Civil Air Transport (CAT) during the French Battle of Diem Bien Phu in North Vietnam.

After the French pulled out of Indochina in 1954, Pope ran charters from Saigon to Taiwan. He was once again called into service by the CIA for CAT in April 1958 to fly B-26 Invader bombers for a clandestine operation known as AUREV, which was called the "Revolutionary Air Force" of Indonesia. He flew to the Philippines to pick-up a B-26, which was painted black. With no identification to indicate what country he was from, which was characteristic of a CIA clandestine operation.

AUREV had taken over an Indonesian Air Force Base in Northern Sulawesi which was the base of operations for CAT. CAT had a small Air Force of about 20 B-26 bombers and C-119 Boxcars. Many of the aircraft were crudely painted with the Nationalist Chinese markings of Taiwan. Even some of the pilots were Nationalist Chinese. Their goal was to destroy shipping going into Indonesia, which would weaken the Indonesian economy and force Sukarno to step down as President. This plan was rather simplistic and poorly thought out, and destined to fail. As Pope and other pilots bombed and sank commercial ships, they also began to bomb military bases on neighboring islands, warehouses and military transport ships and military installations belonging to the Indonesia's military.

As the bombings became more indiscriminate, the CIA decided to change the rules of engagement by only authorizing attacks of airfields and boats. On the morning of May 18, 1958, Pope and his radio man attacked Ambon, which was an Indonesian Air Force base. He then pulled his attention to a ship named "Sweega" and began to fire upon it, but got hit by ground fire and was forced to bail out. He and his radio man landed on a nearby island and were picked up by the Indonesian Navy.

The US Ambassador to Indonesia, Howard Jones, told Sukarno that Pope was a "paid mercenary" and not part of the US Military or any US Clandestine service like the CIA. However, Ambassador Jones couldn't explain why he had flight logs and other damming evidence indicated he was an America pilot recruited by CAT, which was a CIA front.

During his trial he admitted bombing targets on one or two missions, but couldn't explain why his log book indicated he had flown 8 missions. His defense was that he should be treated as a prisoner of war, however, it was rejected and he was being prosecuted as a spy, which would be death. On April 29, 1960, Pope was found guilty of killing 17 members of the Indonesian armed forces and six civilians and was sentenced to death. [61]

Indonesia had irrefutable evidence that the United States, and in particular the CIA, was trying to over throw Sukarno, and they were able to use Pope as a bargaining chip to get military arms from the United States for the release of Pope. After 3 years in house arrest, in Feb of 1962, US Attorney Robert Kennedy flew to Indonesia and negotiated the release of Pope. [61]

As Pope was taken to the Airport in Jakarta for his flight back to the United States, Sukarno told Pope:

"I want no propaganda about it, now go. Lose yourself in the USA secretly. Don't show yourself publicly. Don't give out news stories. Don't issue statements. Just go home, hide yourself, get lost, and we'll forget the whole thing." [61]

After his release from prison in 1962, he returned to Miami, Florida and joined Southern Air Transport (SAT). And yes, as you may have figured out, it was another CIA front organization that flew covert missions in Southeast Asia and Central America. [62]

Sukarno's move toward Socialism

After the Pope affair in the early 1960's, and relations between Sukarno and the United States improved, at least on the surface. Sukarno implemented his socialist agenda by taking control of the media, publishing and enacted anti-discrimination laws against Indonesians by the Chinese. He also dissolved the elected assembly and established a self-appointed assembly. He broke relations with the Netherlands, and confiscated all Dutch owned businesses and private and commercial land.

In the West, the media portrayed Sukarno as a despot, but in reality, he was well respected by the people of Indonesia. He did not have secret prisons and would not allow torture or incarcerate political enemies. By the mid 1960's, he had confiscated assets belonging to foreigners and even the wealthy as he slowly and methodical made his conversion toward communism. By 1965, Sukarno withdrew from the UN Security Council, which meant he was completing his governmental move toward full and complete communism. In September of 1965, he made a speech declaring he was moving to the second phase of the revolution, which was to mean total socialism.

The Indonesian Massacres

On September 30, 1965, Indonesia's top six anti-communist generals were kidnapped, tortured and killed. People suspected the PKI (communist party) was involved in the kidnappings. This event triggered a chain of events which led to the fall of Sukarno's government and the massacre of nearly half million people in Indonesia.

Major General Nasution, escaped death, but his daughter and his aid were killed during the purge. General Suharto, who was a low level military official in the army, now became the Commander of the Army and he ordered all communist and communist sympathizers be purged. By the summer of 1966, as many as one half million were killed. Riots broke-out all over Indonesia and ethnic cleansing of Chinese was reported throughout Indonesia. The reason the Chinese were attacked was that many felt all Chinese were communist and Mao sympathizers.

To this day it is not known who killed the generals, some suspect the PKI communist, others accuse Suharto and yet others accuse the CIA. The truth will never be known. The CIA maintain they were not involved in any covert action related to the purge of 1966 against the communist in Indonesia, while others steadfastly hold that the CIA provided Suharto's military a list of 50,000 communist names to be purged. No solid proof has come forward that implicates the CIA and the overthrow of Sukarno.

Suharto's New Order

After taking control of the government and purging the PKI communist out of government, Suharto became the Supreme Commander as detailed in the Constitution. Suharto didn't want to appear to be a power grabber, so he gradually changed the constitution and slowly gave less and less power to Sukarno. He had already removed General Nasution and placed him under house arrest, and installed a crony parliament until he had enough votes in March 1967 to have Sukarno removed from government and placed under house arrest. The Provisional Peoples Representative Assembly voted Suharto as acting Vice President and in March of 1968, elected Suharto to a five year term as President. Both Sukarno and Major General Nasution died in 1970, while under house arrest.

This paved the way for Suharto, since he had rid himself of all generals, and any opposition within the government. At this point, he was untouchable. The

United States and Britain were indifferent, partly because they got rid of a communist leader and now could trade openly in Indonesia.

Suharto's new order was nothing new at all. He became the ultimate military authoritarian dictator and in no time installed censorship of the media, forbid the freedom of association and assembly, control of the judiciary, and imprisonment of those critical of his regime. To keep control of his political machine, he created two intelligence agencies, "Operational Command for Restoration of Security and Order" and the "State Intelligence Coordination Agency". Reports of torture and imprisonment by his Intelligence agencies were common, but few had the courage to protest. Corruption and nepotism in government was common place in Suharto's Regime, but the United States continued to give economic support and aid to keep Suharto on the side of the United States and Britain. The Western countries had no problem overlooking the human rights violations and turning a blind eye to corruption and crimes against humanity.

The good news was that under Suharto Regime, the Indonesian economy had grown to the point where it was becoming the center for foreign investment. Suharto hired an American economic team to give advice to his administers on how to encourage foreign companies and investors to come to Indonesia. The group was called the "Berkeley Mafia". Suharto privatized almost everything from oil, mining, construction and logging. American and British companies flocked into Indonesia and exploited the opportunity and enjoyed the fact that there were no environmental impact statements, no inspections and no oversight. They could do almost anything they wanted and they didn't have to clean up after they extracted the natural resources. All that was required was to pay Suharto money for the privilege, and the money amounted to billions of dollars. The companies got rich; Suharto got rich and the people and got poorer.

Suharto ruled Indonesia with impunity. He was elected President from 1960 through 1998 in five year terms and unopposed without any opposition. He eliminated all political parties except his own, which was controlled by his military regime. However, political riots were becoming more frequent by 1996. Political opposition groups were immediately arrested and charged with the Anti-Subversion and Hate-spreading laws enacted by Suharto.

His seventh and final re-election was held in March 1998, and as before, he ran unopposed. Riots broke-out and a revolution began against Suharto and his corruption. His support began to wane and even the military began to turn against him and would be asked to resign.

Corruption and Legacy

Suharto was labeled "the greatest kleptocrat of all time". In July of 2000, he was accused of embezzling $571 million of government donations to a number of his personal foundations and was placed under arrest, but later released without legal action. According to Transparency International, Suharto embezzled more money than any other leader in history. They estimated he embezzled between $15 to $35 billion dollars during his 32 year rule. [63]

During his reign, more than a half million were killed in his communist and Chinese purge. He was never charged with crimes against humanity.

The World Bank reports that at least 20% to 30% of Indonesian governments development funds were diverted to government personnel, politicians and senior level government officials, including Suharto himself.

Suharto was never prosecuted for embezzlement or fraud or corruption and was never held accountable for the billions he embezzled. Suharto died January 27, 2008. But even for h criminal acts, he was looked up to by one leader who would become Suharto's mentor, his name was President Ferdinand Marcos and his wife Imelda of the Philippines.

Singapore

Singapore was a British colony for more than 130 years. It was a city state on the lower tip of the Malaysian Peninsula. Both Malaysia and Singapore were colonies of Britain until Malaysia declared its independence after World War II, and Singapore gained full independence from Malaysia in 1965. It became a representative democracy with a constitution, in which the President is elected by popular vote.

During World War II, Britain fortified Singapore with large shore batteries in the event of a Japanese invasion by sea. More than 100,000 British and Australian troops were stationed in Singapore in 1941. However, when the Japanese arrived in 1942, they invaded Thailand and Malaysia and marched troops down the peninsula through Thailand and Malaysia to Singapore. The British was unable to use their big guns, since they were all facing the sea, expecting an invasion from the sea. After 70 days of fighting the British was running out of food and ammunition, 135,000 troops surrendered to the Japanese in February 1942. The captured troops were sent to Changi Prison in Singapore and some were put on "Hell Ships" and sent to Borneo to work as slave labors. The remainder were sent to work on the "Death Railroad" in Thailand and Burma.

Once all prisoners were sent to work on projects throughout Asia, the Japanese began a systematic order of genocide toward the Chinese population called "Sook Ching.

Sook Ching

What is now known is that Japan had already made plans to perform genocide on Chinese and other ethnic groups in Singapore prior to the invasion of Singapore. Sook Ching means "Purge through Cleansing". Japan had a hatred for the Chinese and decided to purge all Chinese in Singapore once they had taken control of the city. The Massacre began on February 18, 1942 and lasted until March 4, 1942, and was later extended into Malaysia as well. Mass executions were performed in numerous cites and along the beaches in Singapore. Almost all were Chinese; however they had a list of other "undesirables" which included: those who had tattoos, those who contributed money to relief efforts in China, those who owned weapons, those who were civil servants, those who were sympathetic toward the British and so on and so forth. The Japanese set up screening centers where all Chinese males between 18 to 50 years old were said to have been purged, either sent to prison or executed. In all, the Japanese claimed they only purged 5,000, but records and burial sites that were exhumed after the war, indicate as many as 40,000 to 50,000 were massacred in Singapore. The exact number will never be known.

Seven Japanese were convicted of war crimes of which, three were executed and four received life sentences. The Japanese who was the master mind of the plan, Tsuji, escaped and fled to China.

Chapter 13

Philippines

Spain claimed the Philippines as a territory in 1542 and was named after Prince Philip of Spain, who later became King Philip II. The Philippines remained under Spanish control for the next 350 year. After the Spanish American War of 1899, Spain ceded the Philippines to the US under the Treaty of Paris in 1899. The first Governor-General of the Philippines was William Howard Taft who served from 1901 to 1904, and would later become the President of the United States in 1908 and the Chief Justice of the US Supreme Court in 1921. In 1934, Congress passed the Tydings-McDuffie Act which provided a transitional period toward independence to the Philippines by 1946. Sergio Osmena would become the first President of the Philippines.

Infamous Ferdinand Marcos

The Philippines has had some colorful leaders since its independence in 1946, however, none more colorful than Ferdinand Marcos. Ferdinand Marcos became the most notorious dictator of all time, not because of crimes against humanity, which he is also guilty of, but because of his greed. Ferdinand Marcos had a life in politics. He passed the Bar exam while on death roll for the murder of his father's political adversary in 1935.

His father, Mariano Marcos was a member of the House of Representatives from 1925 to 1931. He lost the election to Juilo Nalundasan in 1935 for the second time. Two days after the election on September 20, 1935, Juilo

Nalundasan was murdered in his home. Marcos, who was only 18 at the time, along with his father's brother-in-law, Quirino Lizardo, were found guilty of murder in 1939 and sentenced to death. Marcos' godfather, Chua, was the municipal court judge in Batac and pulled some political strings with the Supreme Court Judge, Jose P. Laurel, and all charges dropped in 1940.

When the war broke-out, Marcos served in the Military, however, on March 8, 1945, his father, Mariano Marcos was found to be a Japanese collaborator. The Philippine guerrillas tied each arm to a water buffalo, facing opposite directions, and whipped the buffalo's, thus killing his father. [69]

After the war, Marcos practiced law and some claim he filed false compensation claims for wartime damages against the U.S. Government. One such claim was for $600,000 for 2,000 imaginary cattle of Mariano Marcos (father). [68]

In 1946, Marcos served as special assistant to the first President of the Philippines for one year and served in the House of Representatives from 1949 to 1959 and the Senate from 1963 to 1965. He ran for President of the Philippines in 1965 and won.

Marcos had a cult personality and was popular with the people. In 1969, he won his second term as President, but in 1970, demonstrations and protests gripped the country, which was called the "First Quarter Storm". As the demonstrations continued, Marcos declared martial law in 1972.

The New Society

Marcos admired Indonesian President Suharto and his "New Order" which went into effect when he became President in 1968, just 4 year before Marcos declared his

"New Society". Marcos wrote the book, "Notes on the New Society" which outlines a movement of the poor and the affluent to work together for the common goal of the Filipino people. Under his "New Society", it would extended the presidential term limits, lock the doors of Congress and imposed media censorship, freedom of assembly and curtailed civil liberties of the people.

Marcos ordered the arrest of opposition leaders and established a new Constitution which would change from a Democracy to a Parliamentary dictatorship. This change would allow Marcos to stay in power indefinitely. By 1973, his dictatorship was complete. All opposition was imprisoned and like Suharto, and he became a right-wing authoritarian dictator. Like Suharto, he was able to divert massive amount of cash and gold to his personal off shore accounts and like Suharto. He requested from the United States military and foreign aid which would be unaccounted for and easy to divert. All he needed was some communist insurgents, to convince the United States that he was fight communist insurgents.

As previously mentioned, American foreign policy was centered on anti communist fervor and "Red Fear" reinforced under the Kirkpatrick Doctrine during the Reagan administration. Regardless if the regime was authoritarian or totalitarian, as long as they were anti-communist, America provided financial and military aid in exchange for allowing American businesses to set up shop on foreign soil. Businesses in turn would give kick-backs to regimes; such was the case in the Philippines. It was a perfect formula for fraud and corruption, and it worked well for Suharto and Ferdinand Marcos and other dictators around the world.

Ronald Reagan and Ferdinand Marcos were very close friends, even before he was President and serving as the Governor of California. In 1969, when Reagan was

Governor of California, he and Nancy spent their vacation in the Philippines as guests of the Marcos's. Marcos was generous with the campaign contributions which were in the millions each year while Reagan was running for President.

President Ronald Reagan and Vice President George H W Bush overlooked the fact that he was a dictator. In their eyes he was considered a patriot of democracy, because of his anti-communist posture. The United States couldn't provide foreign aid fast enough into Marcos's Authoritarian Regime. In 1990, Gerry Spence was representing Imelda Marcos in her fraud, racketeering and conspiracy trial in New York, when he told the court that Marcos seized dictatorial control in 1972 because there were 25,000 to 30,000 armed communist. This was a re-occurring theme that Marcos used to justify seizing power, and requesting additional financial aid from the United States, however, CIA estimated that there were only 1,000 communist in the "New People's Army" in the Philippines. Marco claimed that 50 communist insurgents were arrested during the demonstrations of 1971, but all 50 were found to be political opposition leaders such as Benigno Aquino, who would be later assassinated by Marcos's military. [70]

By 1977, more than 60,000 Filipinos had been arrested as political prisoners. In 1981, Vice President George H.W. Bush praised Marcos as a person who:

".....adherence to democratic principles and to the democratic processes"

Obviously he didn't know Ferdinand Marcos that well.

Benigno Aquino Jr. was a political opposition leader and well loved and respected by the entire Philippine population, which was the reason why Marcos had to get rid of him.

During Marcos's declaration of martial law and his new dictatorship in 1972, Benigno Aquino was arrested along with several others and sent to prison. There he remained for nearly eight years. In 1980, while in prison, he had a heart attack and needed medical care, so Marcos permitted him to travel to America for medical treatment. Aquino remained in America for three years when in 1983 he decided to return to the Philippines after hearing that Marcos was having health problems, but found that Marcos refused to give him a passport to travel to the Philippines. He later was able to get a passport through political connections in the Philippines. Marcos then notified all international airlines that they would deny landing rights if Aquino was on their airplane, but under pressure from unknown sources, he had to rescind his order.

When Benigno Aquino arrived at the Manila airport, he was met with a military escort of 25 soldiers and escorted to the aircraft apron. Shortly after, two shots rang out and Aquino and Rolando Galman were dead.

Rolando Galman was the fall guy in the conspiracy and Marcos claimed that Galman assassinated Aquino. The public wasn't buying this wild claim. Marcos arrested the 25 soldiers and cleared all of them by claiming that Galman was the triggerman and acted alone. After Marcos was removed from power in 1986, 16 soldiers were indicted for the murders and sentenced to life in prison. Later the 16 requested a reduced sentence of 22 years because they said the mastermind of the murders was a business partner and crony of Marcos. The trail of the murders always led back to Marcos and his Security General, Fabian Ver.

After the assassinations of Aquino and Galman, the politicians in Washington were scrambling, with hopes that it will all blow over. In 1985 Chief General Fabian Ver was arrested, but was acquitted of all charges for the murder of Aquino. The public considered it a miscarriage of Justice and demonstrations continued. Impeachment hearings of Marcos commenced, claiming Marcos was diverting U.S. aid funds into his personal account. A local newspaper reported that Marcos had large investment properties in the United States, London, Rome, and Hawaii, which was creating a public relations problem for Marcos and his wife Imelda, especially because the Philippine national debt climbed from 2 billion when he took office to over 30 billion dollars. Even though the GNP each year was over 6%, it wasn't enough to offset the national debt. The inflation rate was nearly 50% and the treasury was out of money and was unable to back the peso.

Marcos and the Final Days

By 1984 Reagan wanted to distance himself from Marcos because of a possible political backlash from the assassination of Aquino and his close relationship with him. The Philippines, national newspapers continued to report on Marcos and Imelda's opulent and extravagant lifestyle, especially her collection of 2,700 designer shoes. The Marcos had worldwide investments in foreign banks, mansions and shopping malls and apartment buildings in New York.

By 1986, Washington realized that Marcos was not the soft dictator as they thought and he was baiting America to get foreign aid. Reagan's go-between was Senator Laxalt, a Republican from Nevada, advised Marcos to "cut and run". Marcos and Imelda's money came from kickbacks from American companies doing business in the Philippines, but much of the money came from foreign and military aid to fight communist. After having an election and rigging the votes, he had to leave the Philippine in a hurry with his wife Imelda, but independent observers notice that Marcos rigged the votes.

Demonstrations turned into riots and were threatening to storm the Palace. He contacted his go-between in the U.S., Laxalt and arranged a helicopter to take them to Clark Air Force Base to catch a plane to Hawaii.

When he arrived in Honolulu to his amazement and shock, he had to go through Customs and Immigrations. They had about 250 boxes of personal items, of which, 21 boxes was purported to have been filled with money and 24 gold bricks. The U.S. Custom Service seized $8.2 million dollars.

Marcos's had one of the largest individual collects of art in the world. One Monet painting sold for 30 million dollars. The United States seized over $600 million dollars and returned it to the Philippines. Although he was certainly among one of the biggest thieves, but by no means the biggest, in which that dubious honor goes to his nemesis Suharto of Indonesia.

Cory Aquino won the election in the Philippines; who was Benigno Aquino's wife. She restored democracy in the Philippines and was very popular with the people. Reagan waited two months before he congratulated her by phone on her win over Marcos at the insistence of the White House Staff. Reagan refused to grant Aquino full honors for her visit to Washington in 1986, as was customary under US protocol. For some reason, Reagan refused to accept the fact that Ferdinand Marcos was a dictator who plunder the Philippine treasury and nearly drove the country into bankruptcy.

Chapter 14

American's Foreign Policy in Asia

To understand the reasoning and logic behind America's foreign policy, we must first understand what makes a country want to switch from a democracy to communism or an authoritarianism government to begin with. The answer may surprise you, they don't have a choice or they don't want to change.

The Truman Doctrine

During World War II, the Germany occupied Greece since 1941. As the war was winding down, communist insurgents from Yugoslavia under the leadership of Marshall Tito, became part of the Eastern Europe's communist bloc of states. Britain sent 40,000 troops to Greece in an effort to stop Greece from falling into the hands of the communist. By 1947, Britain could not afford to fight another civil war, especially after World War II, so they elected to pull its troops out of Greece. The United States Congress passed the Truman Doctrine and the Marshall Plan, which became the standard Policy for Containment of Communism and to stop the spread of communism beyond its 1945 borders.

The Marshall Plan was a $400 million aid package for Greece to help them economically. The purpose of the Marshall Plans was to provide aid to countries devastated during the war and provide aid to help rebuild and put people to work so communism couldn't take hold. With the influx of reconstruction funds, it would reduce poverty and unemployment, and thwart communism.

The Truman Doctrine and the Marshall Plan established the basis for U.S. Policy for the next 40 years in an effort to confine communism with the use of money rather than bullets. It was a policy which led America into Indochina in 1961 to thwart the spread of communism in South East Asia. However, the policy eventually morphed into other policies which did not have clear direction or scope.

The United States didn't have much of a foreign policy after World War II except the Truman Doctrine. American leaders disliked colonization and pushed Great Britain, Netherlands and France to give independence to their colonies in Asia and as part of an agreement made during America's entry in World War II as a trade-off for the lend-lease program. It was Americans policy that once colonies became independent, they would gravitate toward democracy and a capitalist economy as the only viable alternative toward individual freedoms and prosperity. In 1945, the Soviets violated Yalta Agreement over Poland, and took aggressive actions in Iran and Turkey. The Truman Administration became increasingly suspicious of Stalin and his expansionist plans.

There were three alternative strategies proposed in the wake of Soviets expansion after World War II;

1) the Isolationism policy in which America returns to the pre-war II policy of isolationism.

2) The Détente policy, designed to establish friendly relations with the Soviet Union and establish trade with the communist countries in Europe and Asia. This policy was supported by the late President Roosevelt.

3) The "Rollback" strategy used by Truman in the Korean War, but after the Chinese Army entered into the fray, Truman didn't want to accelerate the war, and switched to the "Containment" strategy of holding the communist at the 38th Parallel. The containment policy worked well in Korea, but failed miserably in Vietnam, Laos or Cambodia. Perhaps the containment policy had out lived its usefulness.

During the Korea War, General MacArthur disobeyed Truman's order of "containment" and continued to advance American troops into the heart of North Korea, which got MacArthur fired for insubordination. This led to MacArthur's famous speech in Congress in which he said, "Old soldiers never die, they just fade away".

The Strategy of Political War and Corruption

Perhaps one of the most controversial policy decisions in America was the involvement in Vietnam. Vietnam changed the entire foreign policy of America. Now that the war is over, it is easy to point out the mistakes and debate what went wrong. As mentioned in Chapter 6, Kennedy somehow had the intuition that subsequent Presidents and military leaders didn't have. He was well aware that Vietnam was a political nightmare to be avoided. He refused to send ground troops into Vietnam, only advisors. Lyndon Johnson, however, favored the containment policy in Vietnam and military intervention to force peace negotiations, as did Truman in Korea, twelve years before. Military intervention provides the "stick" to force negotiations, rather than a means to win and defeat the enemy. This is an important element, because many military leaders thought the purpose of Vietnam was to defeat the Communist when in fact it was to keep them above the 17 degree parallel.

General Westmoreland, like MacArthur, wanted "military intervention" for the purpose of completely defeating the enemy. He insisted that American troops should be deployed into Laos and cut-off Vietnam's supply routes from China and the flow of war materials bound for South Vietnam via the Ho Chi Minh Trail. It was also Eisenhower's belief that the key to defeating North Vietnam was not Vietnam itself, but Laos.

Wars today are fought using guerrilla warfare of one form or another, as adopted and carried-out by Mao Zedong. Mao's theory of guerrilla warfare was to use agreements and negotiations as a stall tactic with the intent of not honoring them. By western values that would be unacceptable and egregious, but in Asian culture, it is viewed simply a method of winning. This view is also carried-over into their economic system and industry, where corruption in both government and industry is considered part of doing business in a capitalist system.

The Policy of Containment

The Policy of Containment was perhaps the brain child of George Kennan, who was the Charge d'affaires at the US Embassy in Moscow in 1946. He suggested that containment was a good alternative which would take a long time and a great deal of patience, but well worth the effort in the long run. It was the foundation for the Truman Doctrine; however the United States, over time, deviated from Kennan's containment theory of "restraining and confining" in favor of deployment of American troops, called "military intervention", which would be a popular policy with ultra conservatives in Congress. Containing communist aggression and stopping communist aggression requires two separate policy strategies. Containment by using military intervention to confine the enemy to a particular border and perhaps force an armistice or treaty, or option two; use military intervention to aggressively attack and destroy, with the hope of defeating the enemy as we did with Hitler and Hirohito in Japan. In order for the later technique to work it requires taking land in the processes.

The containment strategy doesn't work in all situations, even with military intervention to force compliance. Entering into agreements with an enemy who repeatedly violates agreements is destined to fail. The containment policy only works if both sides honor their commitment and agreement with each other. But many regimes view agreements differently than we do. However, to the aggressor's view point, "the end justifies means", so violating agreements is considered a smart strategy in order to take advantage of a particular situation, which is winning.

The Coup D'état

While America worried about Asia falling like dominos into the hands of communist, most countries were already being taken over by authoritarian governments. Most started as a military coups, yet some started as democracies that morphed into dictatorships, such as Marcos in the Philippines and Syngman Rhee in South Korea.

Most Coup d'états involve a military style take-over of the government, called a military junta. They are the easiest way to take-over a country, because a military general can order troops to seize all branches of government in a bloodless coup to over-throw the government. After seizing power, he can purge any and all potential political and military opposition he feels is a potential threat to his power and authority. After all, the military is run like a dictatorship anyway.

One problem with the military dictatorship is once installed, they seldom can be removed and requires another Coup d'état to remove them. Some countries have so many military coups that 95% of the people have no idea who is running the government. They guarantee their perpetuity by eliminating all elections, public and private assembly and freedom of speech and the press. They even take over the news and install friends and family in key positions within the government. Historically speaking, military leaders almost always make very poor government leaders. Most often the economy stagnates or the people sink into a deeper level of poverty under military leadership.

Once the government has been in power for a while, the dictator becomes convinced that the people are on his side. He may thumb his nose at the rest of the world when he is criticized about his human rights history or pro-socialist meanderings. These types of despots can be very dangerous, partly because they perceive themselves as powerful and above the rule of law and have no regard toward cooperation with other nations.

The United States tolerates certain regimes depending on the political party in control in Washington. A Republican administration does not considers the human rights record of a country as important as long as the regime does not become too friendly toward another socialist or communist country. Allowing American business interest to open trade is a big selling point in normalizing a relationships with oppressive regimes. Democrat administrations consider human rights as a major issues of concern, as well as multiple party elections, rather than a single party. But, we will accept single party dictators as long as we consider them "Freedom Fighters" and have the will and desire to over-throw communist or socialist leaning governments. This was one reason why America and China supported Pol Pot and the Khmer Rouge of Cambodia. It is difficult to say which policy will work, but I speculate it may depend on the person in power. How willing he is to make a change and how defensive is he when suggesting a change. On a policy standpoint, it is important to know and understand the temperament of who you are dealing with.

Rollback

The term "rollback" is a strategy of forcing change in the policies by replacing the ruling regimes. Rollback policy has been used as far back as the American Civil War and Teddy Roosevelt in the Spanish American War and his effort to secure Panama. It was occasionally used for major war events prior to World War II; however it is currently being used against hostile governments not aligned with America's foreign policies, which will depend on the political party in power at the time.

Ronald Reagan was a master of the rollback policy, which became known as the Reagan Doctrine. While the current success rate is low, we continue to use the "Rollback" policy with hopes it will eventually have a favorable outcome. Rollback most always leads to "Blowback", where a terrorist cell attacks foreign countries in retaliation for past failed "Rollback" activities. In most cases, the losers are always aimed at civilians, which are easy targets.

Blowback

"Blowback" is a term coined by the CIA Intelligence Agency for an unintended consequence of a covert operation by an aggressor, usually a terrorist cell, against the United States or one of its allies. "Blowback" usually involves random acts of terror (political) against civilians, as a result of a CIA "Rollback" operation that failed. In many cases, especially in the middle east, what may seem to be a "Blowback" situation is just terrorism in which a particular group or radical discontents wanting to make a statement to fuel the flames of hatred. I suspect much of the blowback today is hate related over the policy of a foreign country.

Foreign Policy toward Dictatorships

A republic is a representative form of government that is ruled according to a charter or a constitution. A democracy is a government that is ruled according to the will of the majority. The people must vote by an electoral process to determine the will of the people, at least in respect to whom they want to represent them in government. There is no true democracy in government, only a representative democracy, such as the United States. It was designed during the construction of America's constitution in 1787 as ratified in 1791, because it would be too difficult to get 150 million people in the Capital Building to vote on every law submitted to Congress.

Dictator's are not democratic and in most cases far from being a republic as they espouse. When it comes to stopping communist aggression, we have the policy of "Containment" and "Rollback" and "Détente". When it comes to dictatorships, our relationships with third world countries, uses a completely different policy formula. Because of America's position toward communism and socialism, we prefer to associate and align ourselves with conservative governments' more than liberal ideology dictators.

The United States "picks and chooses" dictators whom we consider good trading partners. In exchange, we may offer financial and military aid. In general, we usually select regimes that are "right-winged" and demonstrate a conservative ideology. It makes little difference what their history toward human right or their practice toward genocide.

Jean Kirkpatrick was the U.S. Ambassador to the United Nations from 1981 to 1985. She was appointed by Ronald Reagan. Kirkpatrick maintained that:

"Traditional authoritarian governments are less repressive than revolutionary autocracies…..and more susceptible to liberalization ….more compatible with U.S. interests" [64]

In other words, dictators who are authoritarian are preferable and less likely to repress the rights of the people than communist leaning or socialist regimes.

This would be known as the Kirkpatrick Doctrine. Kirkpatrick's theorized that a right-winged authoritarian government was more likely to move from an authoritarian regime to a democratic government than a socialist or communist government to a democracy. Of course we know that this is not true, because the Soviet Union is now a democracy as well as most of the European Bloc countries that were once communist and socialist. Today, there are only 5 countries that are communist and three of which have capitalist economies.

Very few autocratic dictators are willingly to give-up their power to become a democracy, partly because if the people were allowed to vote, they would be voted out. We have twenty-four authoritarian governments in the world today and we spend more money in foreign aid on authoritarian governments than ever before, yet none have made the big leap toward democracy. Most despot regimes have elections but only have a single political party system with one name on the ballot. As for the Constitution, most repressive regimes write a Constitution which only guarantees that their regime remains in power.

America's human rights policy toward foreign countries and authoritarian regimes did not become an issue until the end of the Vietnam War in 1973. The legislative branch wanted a connection between foreign aid and human rights violations by country, which set the stage for a bitter conflict between the legislative branch and the executive branch of government. As previously mentioned, for the most part, Republicans were opposed to using history and on-going acts of human rights violations as a tool to deny financial and military aid to a country, whereas the Democrats wanted to link foreign aid to the country's human rights record.

The International Financial Assistance Act of 1961 and 1977, as amended in 1978 and 1984 by congress, stated that no assistance be given to any country who demonstrated a consistent pattern of gross violation of international human rights. The terminology used in the law was vague, with little meaning and unenforceable. Congresses intent was to enact a strict policy toward not authorizing financial and military assistance to nations who were consistently practicing genocide, imprisonment of political opposition or crimes against humanity, such as Pol Pot, Suharto and Marcos, to name only a few. Nixon and Reagan both argued that during the cold war, it was necessary to have regional security than be concerned about behavioral concerns of our allies, however, congress wanted the United States to distance themselves from all oppressive regimes. [71]

Exporting Democracy

In a democracy, not all countries are capable of implementing and practicing democratic reform; in fact few make the transition. The United States views democracy as people being able to vote and choose who they want to run their government and be represented by them in the law making process. But in reality, voting is just part of what makes democracy work. The United States created a policy of "Exporting Democracy" to third world countries so that they would not be tempted by the trappings of communism or authoritarianism, when times were hard. The technique used was direct intervention by military force, either direct or indirect or by covert or overt intervention. Since dictators rarely vacate their authoritarian position on their own, the only other option was to sponsor pro-democracy leaders or groups called "freedom fighters" who were willing to over-throw a repressive government. America would supply the freedom fighters with military and financial aid to assist in the over-throw.

The "Export Democracy" policy continues today, but didn't enjoy much success, partly because most countries felt that the United States was meddling into their internal affairs, that created even more resentment toward America and its foreign policies, which most always led to "Blow Back".

While the "Export Democracy" concept sounds like a good idea in theory, however in practice, it was more of a clandestine operation of assassination and treachery that had little to do with democracy at all.

Chapter 15

Future Policy in Asia

This book is not about good people wanting to do good things, but rather about bad people doing bad things out of greed and power. Something happens when charismatic leaders get into a positions of power and authority. With few exceptions, the temptation is too great for those who fail to focus on the main goal that brought them into power in the first place.

Foreign policy has changed little over the past hundred years. America has always worked toward globalization of a free market economy for the purpose of expanding markets by importing exporting American products overseas.

For the first time in history we are seeing Communist nations prosper under a capitalist economic system in which, only thirty years ago, the same nations were criticizing western opulence and capitalism. These countries spent little on domestic programs to address poverty, health and social issues that would improve the domestic lifestyle of its people, but elected to spend a disproportionate amount of money on a military and military industrialization for themselves and for export. Most often the military uses their own military on their own people rather than fight foreign invaders. We are living in perhaps the most volatile time in history. Dozens of countries are producing and selling arms and weapons in an effort to balance their trade deficit and boost their military defense. Most of the weapons and military hardware are sold to authoritarian governments and third world countries who support terrorist groups and organizations. The United States being the largest manufacturer of military equipment and hardware continues to supplying countries that we will more than likely be forced to fight at some point in time.

People always want change, especially when living in poverty and see little hope of improving their social status. They reach for a charismatic leader who promises change and the prospects of prosperity and a good life. Dictator's capitalized on broken promises and deceptive practices to sway citizens into believing they have the solution to their problems. In reality, they become the problem, and their greed obscures their ability to see the difference. It becomes obvious that many are oblivious to the difference between those who administer governments and those who control it.

But while we rejoice in having repressive regimes gravitate toward capitalism and a market economy, it may also be a "double edge sword". China and its 2,000 year old empire has long since depleted much of their natural resources. This has forced them to search for natural resources outside their borders, and in doing so, could be a formula for future conflicts. Large countries devour small countries or at least, take advantage of them in one form or another. Such was the case with Japan with the invasion of Korea, Manchuria and China.

These third and second world countries are eager to sell their products to the more affluent western nations at cut-rate prices. To compete, labor intensive manufacturing facilities in the west build plants in less developed nations where labor is cheap and profits are high. It is not about loyalty or patriotism, but rather about profit margins.

The next war in Asia may not involve conventional warfare, but rather a war over trade and financial dominance and who has collected the most marbles. Vietnam is emerging as another industrial nation with cheap labor and following in the footsteps of China in which other Asian nations will soon follow.

America's role in the world should not be the Sergeant of Arms, but rather the caretaker of democracy. We should lead by example rather by force. There will always be nations that cannot be saved from tyranny and oppression, since most nations are not easily adaptable to our form of democracy. Gene Sharp in his book, "Dictatorship to Democracy" said it best;

"The degree of liberty or tyranny in any government is in large degree a reflection of the relative determination of the subjects to be free and their willingness and ability to resist efforts to enslave them"

Footnotes

1 Mao Zedong was raised in an affluent family. His family were landlords and upper middle class farmers, which was contrary to what Mao espoused. Page 19

2 This was the same strategy used in World War II, with the attack on Pearl Harbor on December 7, 1941, just hours before the declaration of War was received in Washington DC. Page 26

3 The name was changed from Nanking to Nanjing after World War II. Nanking was the third largest city in China and the headquarters for Chiang Kai-Shek's Nationalist Army. Chiang Kai-Shek fled Nanking on December 1, 1937, nine days before the Japanese Army arrived. Page 31

4 Some Japanese hotly dispute the Nanking Massacre, but historical documents and photographs substantiated the atrocities committed. Because of the terrible losses sustained in the Battle for Shanghai, the Japanese Army retaliated against the civilian population. Page 32

5 It was during this period (1932-1945) that General Shiro Ishii of Japan, constructed Unit 731 in Northern China and Manchuria for the purpose of developing Chemical and Biological weapons to be used against the Chinese population. Later human experimentation and research was conducted as well. A section in Chapter 4 details the result of his research. Page 37

6 This was the same ploy used by the North Vietnam communist to invade South Vietnam in 1975. Once US Troops pulled out of Vietnam, they violated the Paris Peace Treaty by invading South Vietnam. The foreign aid guaranteed North Vietnam in the Paris Peace Agreement was voided as a result. Page 84

7 This tactic was used during the signing of the peace agreement in 1975, where they failed to purposely deploy communist troops out of the south after signing the peace agreement. Page 115

8 Calley received 3 years under house arrest and received a Presidential pardon by Nixon. Page 131

9 There was no evidence that leaflets were dropped on My Lai or My Khe, as Ramsdell claimed. Page 133

10 Using youths to spy and conduct atrocities against its people was characteristic in both Nazi Germany and Mao's Revolutionary Red Guard. Youths were naïve, malleable and easily swayed. Page 172

11 The United States was intent on having Pol Pot's communist regime return to power. In 1980, U.S. Secretary of State, George Shultz, serving under the Reagan administration, opposed any efforts to bring justice to Pol Pot and the Khmer Rouge for crimes against humanity. James Baker, during the Bush administration also refused to prosecute those responsible. Page 179

References

1) GlobalSecurity.Org/intll/ops/laos Retrieved: Aug. 7, 2015

2) Drug Fallout by Alfred McCoy, Progressive Magazine 1997, Retrieved: Aug. 7, 2015

3) Central Intelligence Agency, CIA Air Operations in Laos, 1955-1974 William M. Leary, Retrieved: Aug. 8, 2015

4) Berkeley Daily Planet, Dispatches from the Edge: Vang Pao, Drugs and the CIA, Conn Halliman, 01/12/2011

5) Frontline #613, Air Date 05/17/1988, Produced and Written by Andrew and Leslie Cockburn, Directed y Leslie Cockburn, Retrieved, Aug. 3, 2015

6) Spartacus Educational (online), Anthony A. Poshepny (Tony Poe), Retrieved: Aug. 3, 2015

7) Primary Sources: Evan Thomas, The Very Best Men (1995); David Corn, Blond Ghost: Ted Shackley and the CIA Crusades (1994); Alfred W. McCoy, The Politics of Heroin: Complicity in the Global Drug Trade (1972); Richard S. Ehrlich, Asia Times, 7/8/2003

8) The Secret War in Laos, Plain of Jars, Fred Branfman, (1972, Retrieved: Aug. 8 2015

9) China's Last Emperor, Kallie Szczepanski

10) Remembering Taiwan's White Terror by Julie Wu, 3/8/2014 "The Diplomat"

11) The Gang of Four, Website: About Education, by Kallie Szczepanski, Retrieved: Aug. 4, 2015

12) Burchett, William G. and Norodom, Sihanouk (1973). *My War with the CIA: Cambodia's fight for survival.* United States of America: Penguin Books. ISBN 0140216898. I

13) Osborne, Milton E (1994). *Sihanouk Prince of Light, Prince of Darkness.* Honolulu, Hawaii, United States of America: University of Hawaii Press. ISBN 978-0-8248-1639-1.

14) Jeldres, Julio A (2005). *Volume 1–Shadows Over Angkor: Memoirs of His Majesty King Norodom Sihanouk of Cambodia.* Phnom Penh Cambodia: Monument Books. ISBN 974926486X.

15) Corfield, Justin J. (1994). *Khmers stand up! – A history of the Cambodian government 1970-1975.* Centre of Southeast Asian Studies, Monash University. ISBN 0732605652.

16) Norodom Sihanouk, *My War with the CIA*, Random House, 1973,

17) CIA and Operation Phoenix in Vietnam, Ralph McGehee, 1962, Website: Serendipity 2001, Retrived: Aug.4, 2015

18) The Berkeley Daily Planet, Dispatches from the Edge: Vang Pao, Drugs and the CIA, Retrieved: Aug4, 2015

19) The Phoenix Program, CIA's Killer Squads to Eliminate the Viet Cong, Douglas Valentine, Chapter 24

20) Wreaking Havoc One Round At A Time, American Rifleman, Major John L. Plaster, May 2008 , Retrived: Aug. 6, 2015

21) Spartacus-educational.com, John Simkin January 2015 Retrived: Aug,18, 2015

22) Moyar, Mark (2006) Triumph Forsaken: The Vietnam War, 1954-1965' p 272 Cambridge University Press. ISBN 0-521-86911-0, New York

23) "Ngo Dihn Biography" Spartacus Schoolnet.com.uk, revised October 26, 2012

24) B. Diem and D. Chanoff, "In the Jaws of History" p. 100-102

25) The Pentagon Papers. Vol. 2 Ch4. "Overthrow of Ngo Dinh Diem, 1963, pp 201-276

26) How Communism Works, by Alia Hoyt, Retrieved: Aug 8, 2015

27) Asia For Educators, Columbia University, "The Long March", 2009 http://afe.easia.columbia.edu Retrieved: Sept. 2, 2015

28) The Guardian, No. 34 1990, Covert Action, Jack Colhoun, "U.S. Supports Khmer Rouge"

29) Third World Traveler, Uncle Sam and Pol Pot, John Pilger, Covert Action Quarterly, Fall 1997 issue Retrieved: Aug. 28, 2015

30) Wikipedia.com, Khmer Rouge, Weitz, Eric D. (2005). "Racial Communism: Cambodia under the Khmer Rouge". Retrieved: Aug. 27, 2015

31) Who supported the Khmer Rouge?, Oct. 16, 2014, Gregory Elich, Retrieved: Aug. 29, 2015

32) Jack Wheeler, "Robin Hood Commandos Battle Odds in Cambodia, Washington Times, Aug. 10, 1984

33) Charivat Santaputra (1985) Thai Foreign Policy 1932-1946, Thammasat University Press, ISBN 974-335-091-8

34) Wikipedia.com, Communist Party of Thailand, "http:// Wikipedia.org/communist party of Thailand Retrived Aug. 20, 2015

35) Thailand, A Short History, David K. Wyatt, second edition 2003, ISBN 974-9575-44-x Silkworm Books, Chiang Mai

36) David Wilson, The United States and the future of Thailand, (New York 1970) p144

37) Arne Kislenko, Asst. Professor of History, Ryerson University

38) Spartacus Educational.com, John Simkin, March 1953, **www.spartacus-educational.com**, "The Great Purge" Retrieved Aug. 18, 2015

39) "The Treaty of Portsmouth, An Adventure in American Diplomacy, 1969, Eugene P. Trani

40) Wikipedia.com, Russo-Japanese War, Erols.com, Death Tolls and Casualty Statistics of Wars, Dictatorships and Genocides, Retrieved Sept. 5, 2015

41) Fujiwara, Akira (1995), "Nitchu Senso ni Okeru Horyotoshido Gyakusatu" Kikan Senso Sekinin Kenkyu 9:22

42) Judgment International Military Tribunal for the Far East, Paragraph 2, P. 1012

43) Yang, Celia (2006), "The Memorial Hall of the Victims of the Nanking Massacre: Rhetoric in the Face of Tragedy p 310

44) Wikipedia.com, Nanking Massacre, Massacre Contest, main article, Contest to kill 100 people using a sword, citing, Wakabayashi 2000, p. 319, Retrieved, Sept. 13, 2015

45) Cook, Haruko Taya (1992)," Japan at war: An oral history" (1 ed) New York, NY, New Press P. 162 ISBN 1-56584-014-3. As told to: Wikipedia, Unit 731, Retrieved Sept. 15, 2015

46) Christopher Hudson (March 2, 2007, "Doctors of Depravity" Daily Mail, Retrieved: Sept. 15, 2015 www.Wikipedia.com/ Unit 731

47) Barenblatt, David. "A Plague Upon Humanity: the Secret Genocide of Axis Japan's Germ Warfare Operation, Harper Collins, 2004. ISBN 0-06-018625-Retrieved Sept. 15, 2015: www.Wikipedia.com/ Unit 731, Retrieved: Sept. 12, 2015

48) Neuman, William Lawrence (2008). "Understanding Research", Pearson/Allyn and Bacon, P. 65 ISBN 0205471536, Retrieved: Sept. 15, 2015, www.Wikipedia.com/ Unit 731

49) Hal Gold, Unit 731 Testimony, (2003), p 109, Tuttle Publishing, New York, (2006) p.50, (2011) P94 to 97, ISBN 9781462900824

50) http://geography.about.com/od/economic-geography/fl/The-Golden-Triangle.htm

51) Connaughton, R. Pimlott, J, and Anderson, D, (1995), The Battle of Manila, London, Bloomsbury Publishing, ISBN 0891415785, as read (2015) Wikipedia.com/Battle of Manila, Manila Massacre, paragraphs 2, 3, 4 Retrieved: Sept. 3, 2015

52) "Juche Ideology", Columbia School of Law, website, 2015 paragraph 6, Retrieved: Sept. 20, 2015

53) "Weapons of Mass Destruction: Plague as Biological Weapons Agents" GlobalSecurity.org Retrieved September 23, 2015

54) 1978 US diplomatic cable analyzing a news report about the 8 POW killed in Hiroshima, Retrieved Sept. 24, 2015

55) "Japanese Medical Atrocities in World War II, Unit 731" Forum on War Crimes & Redress, Tokyo, Japan 12-11-1999. Sheldon H. Harris Professor of History Emeritus, Calif. State University, Northridge Feb. 25, 2000

56) www.Wikipedia.com/ Unit 731, Retrieved: August 12, 2015

57) Japan unearths sited linkd to human experiments, http://www.theguardian.com/world/2011/feb21/japan-excavates-sites-human-experiments, Retrieved: August 4, 2015

58) Japan Times News, (August 14, 1998, "Green Cross founder tied to Unit 731 preservation" Retrieved: Sept. 25, 2015.

59) The Telegraph, United Kingdom, "Human bones could real truth of Japan's Unit 731 experiments", Julian Ryall, (Feb. 15, 2010) Retrieved: Sept. 25, 2015

60) "Unit 731 Nightmare in Manchuria" Youtube, https://www.youtube.com/results?search_query=unit+731+nightmare+in+manchuria. Bostan Republic Documentary by Shira Shimona

61) Kahin & Kahin 1997, p. 180,181,182 : Retrieved: 2/30/2015, **www.Wikipedia.com/**Indonesia/Sukarno

62) Conboy &Morrison, 1999, p. 166, Retrieved: 2/30/2015, www.Wikipedia.com/Indonesia /Sukarno

63) Aspinal (1999), P. ii, Retrieved 9/30/2015, **www.Wikipedia.com/**Suharto

64) Policy Analysis, Cato Policy Analysis No. 58, "The United States and Third World Dictatorships: A Case for Benign Detachment" by Ted Galen Carpenter, (Aug. 15, 1985) Retrieved: Oct. 7, 2015.

65) www.Wikipedia.com/Atomicbomb, Retrieved Oct 2, 2015, Atomic bombing of Hiroshima and Nagasaki

66) Gowing 1964, pp 40-43, 76-79

67) Jones 1985, pp 7, 89, 82-84, 522, 511-516

68) Ferdinand Marcos, by Kallie Szczepanski, Asian History Expert, Retrieved: Oct. 10, 2015

69) Mariano Marcos, Wikipedia, Lapham R, and Norling B, 1996, Lapham's Raiders, Lexington: U. Kentucky Press, ISBN 0813119499

70) "Defense Says Marcos Heeded Bush's Advice", Los Angles Times, April 4, 1990, William C. Rempel, Retrieved: Oct. 10, 2015

71) Crabb, Cecil V. Pat Holt (1992), Invitation to Struggle: Congress, the President and Foreign Policy, 2 ed. Michigan Quarterly. Pp187-211, ISBN 978-0-87187-622-5, www. Wikimedia.com, Retrieved: Oct 15, 2015

72) The Oxford Companion to American Military History, Oxford University Press 2000, by Guenter Lewy, Retrieved; Oct. 23, 2015.

73) Seymour Hersh, Cover-up (New York: Random House, 1972 Pg. 88 to 95

74) The House Un-American Activities Committee: The History and Legacy of Congress. Charles River Editors, Chapter 2: Hollywood Ten

75) Massacre at Hue http://en.wikipedia.org/wiki/massacre at Hue , retrieved March 1, 2016

76) Hidden Horrors of Vietnam's Re-education Camps by Dennis Rockstroh, April 02, 2005 Posted by Le Quang Duc

77) Cu Chi and Vinh Moc Tunnels, Wikipedia, Retrieved 3-6-2016

78) Bou Meng, A Survivor from Khmer Rouge Prison S-21, by Huy Vannak, Document Center of Cambodia, retrieved 3-9-2016

79) General Ne Win, http://en Wikipedia.org/wiki/General Ne Win/ retrived April, 15, 2016

80) Corfield (a), Justin (2009). The History of Cambodia. Santa Barbara: ABC CLIO. *ISBN 978-0-313-35722-0.* p. 109

81) "George Will Confirms Nixon's Vietnam Treason" by Bob Fitrakis and Harvey Wassserman, retrieved May13,2016

Photos Credits

Cover Photo   Shutterstock/294095897/Strelov

Fig 1	Shutterstock 251930659/Everett Historical
Fig 1a	U.S. Army map, Public domain
Fig 2	Shutterstock 242821915/Everett Historical
Fig 3	Shutterstock 249573598/Everett Historical
Fig 4	Shutterstock 251930671/Everett Historical
Fig 5	Shutterstock 251930449/Everett Historical
Fig 6	Long March_iDO.3MT.Com.Cn
Fig 7	Shutterstock 75114505/Thor Jorgen Udvang
Fig 8	Shutterstock 238057867/Everett Historical
Fig 8a	Flickr CC Manhhal, 1964, Creative Commons
Fig 9	Flickr CC Tommy Japan, Creative Commons
Fig 9B	Flickr CC Manhhal, Luong Nghia/Patrick Chauvel Foundation, Creative Commons
Fig 9C	Flickr CC Manhhal, Creative Commons
Fig 10	Far North Photography/ Doug Beaudoin
Fig 11	Shutterstock 24766159/Moonbeam
Fig 12	Far North Photography/ Doug Beaudoin
Fig 13	Far North Photography/ Doug Beaudoin
Fig 14	Shutterstock 119784799/Matyas Rehak
Fig 15	Shutterstock 70815181/grubaa
Fig 16	Shutterstock 79447375/getiT

Author

Douglas Beaudoin is a lifelong Alaskan and an avid student of history. He spent 4 years in the U.S. Navy in 1966 to 1970, two years of which in Southeast Asia. He retired in 2000 from Alaska Dept. of Transportation and spends much of his time in Asia and learning about Asian culture and history. He lives in the Copper Valley Region in Alaska and is currently working on several nonfiction books about Alaska and American History.

The author (left) with Bo Meng at S-21 Prison, Cambodia

Mr. Meng was one of only seven survivors in Cambodia's S-21 prison, out-of the 16,000 killed, including his wife and children.

His book: "A Survivor from Khmer Rouge Prison S-21"

A Policy of Hate